ELIZABETH WILSON was born in Devon in 1936, and
educated at St Paul's Girls' School and Oxford University,
where she studied English Literature. For some years she
worked as a psychiatric social worker, but since 1973 she
has taught at the North London Polytechnic, and is now
Senior Lecturer in Applied Social Studies there. For the
past ten years Elizabeth Wilson has been actively involved
in the women's movement, the gay movement and left
politics generally. Her first book, *Women in the Welfare
State,* was published in 1977, and in 1980 she published her
second, *Only Halfway to Paradise,* an account of women in
Britain between 1945 and 1968. A member of the editorial
board of *Feminist Review,* she has written for a number of
journals and magazines. She lives in London, and is
working on a new book.

A unique autobiographical book, *Mirror Writing* questions
the assumption implicit in some feminist thinking that if
women 'find a voice' and 'speak out' they will have found
their identity. Suggesting that the idea of 'self' is more
problematic, the author explores autobiography and fiction,
sexuality, psychoanalysis, language and symbolism, as
well as popular books and magazines, in an attempt to
describe the construct   its
contradictions.

For
MARY

MIRROR WRITING

An Autobiography

ELIZABETH WILSON

Published by VIRAGO PRESS Limited 1982
Ely House, 37 Dover Street, London W1X 4HS

Copyright © Elizabeth Wilson 1982

Printed in Great Britain by litho
at the Anchor Press, Tiptree, Essex

British Library Cataloguing in Publication Data
Wilson, Elizabeth
  Mirror Writing.
  1. Wilson, Elizabeth
  2. Feminists—England—Biography
  I. Title
  305.4′2′0924   HQ1595.W/
  ISBN 0-86068-241-2

'Only he who can view his own past as an abortion sprung from compulsion and need can use it to full advantage in the present. For what one has lived is at best comparable to a beautiful statue which has had all its limbs knocked off in transit, and now yields nothing but the precious block out of which the image of one's future must be hewn.'–

Walter Benjamin: *One-Way Street*

I should like to acknowledge particularly the help and support of Ursula Owen, my editor, who sustained me with her confidence in my efforts to write.

E.W.

One

The past is a dream. 1971: I roam Victoria Park in London's East End. I follow the path that skirts the edge. There are families with prams, a glittering lake, a distant grove of trees. The panorama quakes with heat beneath a violet sky. Flying my flag of identity I prowl in search of the demonstration, incognito still, alone, but aware, visible, in yellow tee shirt, blue jeans, high heels.

The demonstration gathers in the centre of the park. When I join the 200 women and men, when we sing, shout and perform our street theatre, my identity expands into the group identity with its subjective sense of potency, the clenched-fist-holding-a-flower of the cultural revolution.

Later, a few of us ride the top of a bus to Hampstead Heath and descend on the quiet retreat of the Ladies' Pond. Our arrival disturbs the peace as we bum cigarettes from the scattered groups of women sitting on the grass in the lengthening shadows. We throw ourselves into the lake, our splashing the sound of pistol shots; laughter in the empty air. Later an Indian meal, and we search in vain for a party.

It was not until I became involved in radical political movements that I ever felt I lived fully in the present or was fully myself. All those years before I'd felt that my identity was suppressed, that I was confined to some self-created psychic prison. What was I? I didn't know. I had not 'found myself'. I looked in all the wrong places, of course–that was my psychic prison, if there was one, a house of mirrors. In every encounter I saw a reflection of myself, distorted, unreal, untrue, yet inescapable, an acute self-consciousness marbled with the unconscious seeping through.

1

My lover, even, whom I did love, was either caught up in this multiple mirroring, or excluded from it—beyond the mirror, through the window—and, for much of the time could only act as a mixture of midwife and onlooker as I struggled to give birth to impossible selves.

Who was that solemn fifties girl, and that enamelled butterfly of the mid-sixties? When I think about that strange, lost era, the Affluent Society, and of 'myself' or rather my lost selves within it, it seems like some weird film or novel, that world of *before*—before the seventies, before women's liberation, before Northern Ireland and the miners' strike and the Grunwick picket and the National Front and Brixton. When I look back it seems like a world of fantasy in which I myself, the politicised self of today, could surely not have *been*. It must have been another self—a horde of other identities.

When I began to write this book I had a dream in which I was looking through a window at a park. The window was veiled with a net curtain. In the park, which seemed at one moment near, at the next far away, was a loved friend. I was trying to get from behind the window into the park, to where she was.

Afterwards I told the dream to the friend who had appeared in it, and as I recalled the dream I understood that the dream park was the park that had stretched out across the road from my first home, in Exeter. From the front window I had often stared through the net curtain at the park, had watched the children and adults strolling, running, playing, seen the pavilion, the tennis courts, even the more distant bowling green with its stooping white figures, and beyond that the swings of the playground. Sometimes I watched with the naked eye, and children, grown ups, dogs and buildings appeared toylike, sometimes I watched through my grandfather's telescope, which magically enlarged the toytown figures into recognisable human beings. To write of that childhood now is to look

2

down the telescope again–to try to get back into the park of my childhood.

*

I was born in the year of the Abdication. Women in white with sculptured hair and men in tuxedos danced the tango on an ocean-going liner. The labels on my mother's luggage forever after said: P & O–Not Wanted on the Voyage–Cabin–State Room.

I was born into a section of the middle class that was shortly to become extinct as the Imperial power it served disintegrated beneath it. Cramped memories of Empire surrounded me in a surburban semi. A crocodile's skull hung on the wall like a symmetrical, dried-up sponge. A leopard-skin rug complete with fangs in a pink wax mouth, with claws and tail, sprawled over the chintzes. My grandmother kept her sewing in an elephant's foot hollowed into an intricate box. Outside it was covered with prickly hair and had huge toenails, inside it was all delicate wood and padded satin. There were leatherwork 'pouffes', brass ashtrays and dusty black ebony carved into angular figurines. My mother kept an ancient stone fertility goddess, a small pot-bellied thing with a face like the Ugly Duchess, on her tiled chimneypiece. But I was her only child.

I played with three black elephants of diminishing size, on the floor. Behind them stalked a thin brass figurine with pointed breasts balancing on her head a flat basket to be used as an ashtray. The procession passed in front of the blue and white chintz which was Chinese in inspiration, or reminiscent of Indian paisley perhaps–a bit of both, in fact, and as much suited to our Empire heritage, our hegemony over the world.

The adults stared round me, talking: 'In the old days ...' was my grandmother's phrase; 'Out in the Tropics ...' said my mother, still dressed in her tussore suit.

My grandfather suffered from asthma: 'Confound this

wheezing.' He took me up to the field at the top of the road. High on his shoulders I squeezed my arms round his face when the cow bellowed. Another memory of being hoisted on his shoulders–we went into the country to buy fruit from a farm. He lifted me on to his shoulders so that I could pick a single jewel-like plum from its bough. A globe of brilliant yellow-green, it seemed to be the forbidden fruit I might pick when he lent me the omnipotence of his height.

My grandfather had been born in New Zealand, but was Scottish. He had sailed round the world by the age of twelve.

With the freedom of the whole globe in the hinterland of their past, they were mournful, exiles. They clustered round me. I was the centre of their attention. In the everlasting light evenings of the war I lay in bed. A screen stretched along the wall beside me. The cotton curtains on their wooden frame were printed with Mabel Lucy Atwell figures, peculiar, swollen little girls with orange cheeks. I invented a radio programme about them and lay in bed singing at the top of my voice. My mother came and sat on the stairs outside my room and entreated me to go to sleep. But I went on singing, and she would never come into the room.

One evening I got out of bed and stood on the window sill. I leant against the wooden bars that had been put there to prevent my falling out of the window. I waved and shouted and beamed down from a great height at the adults standing on the lawn: 'Oh–get away from the window, you'll hurt yourself,' cried my grandmother. But I beamed and smiled triumphant: it was *me*. I was there.

When my mother pushed me in my push chair down the road to the park the man next door called: 'Hello Chatterbox' as I passed. I waved to Mr Williams and his white chow, Kim.

During the hot summer of 1976 I returned to Exeter with the friend who was later to appear in my dream of the

4

park. We walked 'down the alleyway' that led from the main road to the road where I had once lived. My friend was surprised that I found it so easily, walking without hesitation back into my personal stone age.

And there, becalmed, were the flat, smiling, suburban houses, the park and the pavilion. Nothing had changed. There was the past stuck against the present in the golden varnish of the motionless, time-warp heat: the land of Chatterbox.

*

I was proud of my gas-mask, a grown up one, not a silly Mickey Mouse one for babies. I had a siren suit like Winston Churchill–a boiler suit but made out of dressing gown material. We still went to Sidmouth for our holiday, and I trailed along the cold stony beach with Billy, my baby doll, in his finery of lacy pink or white, for my mother had knitted him two sets of long dresses and jackets, like a real baby. We walked up the red cliffs or took the blue and cream bus along the coast. We visited Miss Fisher, where I was mesmerised by two objects much more wonderful to play with than my ordinary dolls and farm sets. Miss Fisher had crocheted a rug of purple and green squares, interspersed with other colours, which was draped across her chaise longue; and she had a solitaire board set with the most wonderful marbles, each different, many-coloured.

I possessed a third wonderful toy, a wooden sword, made for me by my grandfather. He had painted the handle gold, the blade silver. I chased through the park with it, leading two little boys, who were my friends. Later it broke and my grandfather replaced it with one even more magnificent, for it had a purple 'jewel' set in the centre of the handle, flanked with smaller red and topaz stones. But I grumbled because he'd painted the handle yellow instead of gold. I remember his anger and hurt, and even at the time I wished, desperately, that I hadn't been so ungrateful.

My grandfather used to visit the Colonels. He put on his

suit of spongebag checks and his panama hat; lean as a piece of string and six feet tall he escorted my mother and myself to tea with the Colonels. She and I also dressed in our best, she in her suit of grey flannel, I in my voile dress of which even the shadow was transparent. It had a frill and raspberry coloured flowers on it and with it I wore a straw hat that was also decorated with red and white flowers. To visit Colonel Brown we went out into the country. There was a grey stone house. The Colonel's wife floated down the wide stairs. She was silhouetted against a great window and dressed in lavender. Colonel Brown gave me a nectarine plucked from their kitchen garden wall. Its smooth skin felt strange–human. Peaches have fur on the skin, but nectarines are hairless, I learned.

We visited Colonel and Mrs Morwhinnie. Again the transparent shadow of my dress on the pavement went before me. Mrs Morwhinnie gave us heavy cakes which made me ill.

It was always the three of us, my grandfather, my mother and I. My grandmother always stayed at home.

*

My mother placed a single square of milk chocolate on the scrubbed wood of the kitchen table: 'This is the last milk chocolate there'll be until after the war,' she said. I decided that I did not like milk chocolate. The chocolate machines had a notice stuck inside them, which read: 'Empty for the duration of the War.' The mournfully admonitory note of this announcement filled me with anguish. When would it end? Didn't anyone know? Pre-war (in the old days . . .)– postwar, we were caught between the two. My mother and grandparents stared at the little maps in the *Daily Telegraph*. The maps had thick, short, black arrows all over them.

A German plane came down in a field. We were taken to see it. There was a black cross on its side. Its window was made of broken plastic. 'But where's the pilot?' I asked, disappointed. Silence.

6

There was an air raid. There were Morrison shelters and Anderson shelters. One was a hut in the garden with a corrugated roof. The other was a sort of cage under the dining table. This I believed to be an Anderson shelter, because our friends the Andersons owned one of this type. We ourselves simply sat behind the garage cuddled in eiderdowns, although it was another hot summer night. It was like fireworks. 'You can see the incendiary bombs over in Southernhay,' they said. And it was true. The sky had turned red. To be up at night–it was wonderful. I laughed, sang and talked. But to this day the sound of planes flying overhead at night frightens me.

When my father came home from Africa we went to stay at the Rougemont Hotel. In the Rougemont gardens were some large, ugly birds called Muscovy ducks, sent by the Russians as a special gesture of goodwill to Exeter. There were Free Poles staying in the Rougemont. The thought of these Poles who were so free was an exciting one, but an air of slight alarm hung over their presence too. They were better by far, though, than the Evacuees who gave you impetigo (tiger?) if you went too near them, and were so stupid that they did not like real cream but only wanted to eat tinned salmon. My mother would always hurry on, dragging me by the hand, if we chanced upon an Evacuee on Heavitree Hill. The Evacuees had the mark of Cain on them, the gentian violet that splodged their faces and limbs.

In the lounge of the Rougemont Hotel they had gilded cane armchairs. With the other child in the hotel, a little boy, I was put to bed downstairs in an improvised bed made from the gilded cane chairs. This was because there was another Raid. Late in the night my grandparents appeared, long-faced. They said they had had to walk all the way, treading everywhere on broken glass. They seemed like two thin, medieval saints in their drooping black clothes, walking on glass in sacrificial penance, a proof of love.

My mother and I shared a double bedroom at the

Rougemont Hotel. This arrangement was repeated when we stayed at a hotel on Dartmoor. There my father had a little red room in the top of a turret, while my mother and I shared a room on the first floor, which had twin beds with pale green eiderdowns that were slippery and slid to the floor.

At the Rougemont Hotel my father became friendly with Miss Coffee. Miss Coffee had a shiny-smooth black pageboy hairstyle and shiny red nails. She bathed me one evening, and gave me a powder puff attached to an artificial silk handkerchief printed in pink and yellow. I told my mother how much I loved Miss Coffee. I was a sucker for her glamour.

The war was a list of names: Dunkirk, Alamein, Tripoli, the Near East, the Middle East, the Far East–the whole globe again. The names were intoned by the wireless which rested on a table next to the armchair in which my slippered grandfather curled sideways for a nap and later listened to the six o'clock news–six bleeps from the brown and golden bakelite box, the news–strings of names, the football results (or was that only after the war?)–strings of names yet more romantic–Tranmere Rovers ... Partick Thistle ... Heart of Midlothian.

My grandfather was in the Home Guard. My mother was in the Women's Voluntary Service, which organised clothing parcels for prisoners of war and refugees, and canteens and entertainments for soldiers stationed in the area. I do not remember what she did–she wore the grey-green uniform, embroidered in maroon. My father administered in Sierra Leone. It was a quiet war.

*

The London house was narrow and dark. The war was over. Each day I took my clean plate to school in a paper bag, and returned with it dirty to be washed at home. This was the Fuel Crisis. 'They'–the diabolical Labour Government–might requisition our house. 'They' might prevent my mother from sending me to a 'good school'.

We dwelt amongst peeling vistas of stucco. West Indian children played on the stairs and in the porches of the cavernous houses further down the road. My grandfather returned from a stroll one day with triumphant news: 'Saw a chap in the next road with a Leander tie'—a fellow exile, my grandfather guessed, in these mean streets, when he spotted the pink tie of the Varsity rowing man.

I came home from school to find the house in darkness. In the dusk my mother appeared through the gloom: 'poor old Grandpa, he's in hospital.' I wanted my tea. My mother was angry in a way that was unfamiliar: 'There's no time for that.' It was the first time I'd ever been in the city at night. There were lights everywhere, a gleaming, noisy blackness. It was dark, but it was like daytime—exciting.

This was University College Hospital. We plunged up stone stairs that wound round a lift like a cage: 'Wait here.' I sat on a bench and gazed at the pattern in the mosaic floor.

In the morning my mother told me he was dead. I was embarrassed by my inability to cry. My mother, I could see, found it unnatural.

*

My father came home with his arm in a sling. Playing bridge on board ship in a storm he'd been flung across the deck. I should have preferred it to be a war wound. He took me on a long journey to see friends of his. We returned in a taxi. He gave me a wet kiss and a pound note. I felt awkward.

He was to make his 'last tour'. We sat in the foyer of the Trocadero, waiting for my uncle, and my father ordered a Gin and It. When it came, he gave me the cherry from it. We dined in a room with murals. I ate a mixed grill and blackcurrant ice cream. A chorus girl with fishnet stockings presented my father with a tray from which he selected a primrose-coloured packet of cigarettes, State Express 555.

We lunched at the Royal Empire Society. There was a huge room dominated by an enormous oil painting of a pride of lions who looked down on us with mournful resignation. The administrators were flocking home from the Empire. My father's life dwindled to bored domesticity, local affairs in Putney and drinks at the tennis club on Sunday.

At school no one understood what my father was, or why he was retired. The world of my school was a London world in which the British Empire had no importance. They talked about art and ballet. I was different. My mother was on her own, and we were poor.

Genteel poverty is different from the grinding poverty of the really poor, for it entails no threat to life, although it does sometimes to health, but it smells of shame and bereavement. We were forever mourning a lost colonial and gentrified status. Real bread-line poverty may give birth to a sense of worthlessness and failure, a sense of being ground down, of being nothing, or to a sense of pride at surviving. Middle-class poverty suggests exile and incompetence. Exiled from her rightful status as a married woman of her class, my mother read the many memoirs then appearing of exiled royalty–kings and queens of Greece, of Rumania, and of Bulgaria, grand dukes and wandering baronesses casting back longing looks at a lost Ruritania. My mother too had her Ruritania in the lost 'out in the tropics' world of the thirties–she who would never swim when we went to the seaside because the water was so cold in comparison with the African Ocean.

My mother was also exiled from adulthood. She smoked cigarettes in our bedroom, on the sly, hiding from her parents, who referred to us as 'the children'. Certain tunes made her cry–the theme song from *La Traviata, Abide with Me*. I came to dread the strange, poignant, awful feeling associated with them. My grandmother used to say to me: 'When you're older you'll understand.' But I already understood and shrank from the dank atmosphere of unhappiness. There was a skeleton in the cupboard. My mother had been mysteriously *wronged*.

My father drove me across Wimbledon Common and we stopped near a woman standing at a corner. My father spoke to her, and introduced me. A little while later I learned that she had become my stepmother.

*

In the dark house hung the crocodile skull, the poison arrows that had once belonged to African huntsmen, the family portraits. Even in the summer the house was dark, although then it had a watery feeling as greenish light filtered into the rooms. At the top of the house lived a series of lodgers. The ground floor was furnished with large antiques. In the basement my grandmother, clothed in black, sat in a deckchair by the kitchen stove with its old-fashioned flue and white-tiled surround. Even in the summer she stoked the fire, murmuring: 'It's cold–oh, *bitterly* cold.' Her deckchair was covered with rugs and cushions as if she were on the voyage to Africa. She was always tired, and her head ached. After she had read everything in the paper, she crossed her arthritic hands and waited patiently for me to return from my girls' school, my mother from her fundraising work. On our return, her long, celtic, gipsy face lit into a sweet, patient smile. She discussed the day's news, and told endless stories of her childhood, of her parents, brothers, sister, grandfather and alcoholic aunt in a huge house with many servants 'before we lost our money'. For her, exile had begun long ago.

The kitchen was covered with mementoes and curios, with 'sayings' and news items cut from the newspaper, and with photographs of Winston Churchill (but later she grew tired of admiring him). The basement passage was lined with tin trunks on which my grandparents' name was painted in white copperplate. The basement smelt cleanly of the boracic powder my grandmother used instead of

11

talc, since she disliked anything scented. Our bath was in the scullery, and I dried myself between a huge mangle and the gas cooker.

I devoted much energy to the attempt to conceal, even to deny, the existence of this strange home. From it I emerged to pose as a normal teenager of the 1950s.

Two

Of the many photographs my grandfather took of me, my favourite shows me on the beach at Sidmouth. It is wartime, 1940. The whole picture has slipped. In the background the dark, shelflike cliff tilts sideways and the flimsy bungalows perched on it have started to slide gently and slowly down the sloping coastline in the direction of Lyme Regis.

I remain upright and, stoically ignoring the impending disaster behind me, I am squatting on a rock, my shrimping net held at the ready. Long, fat ringlets frame my face. I am not looking like my beaming Chatterbox self, for I am staring at the camera with reproach and anxiety, serious and distrustful. I am four years old, and while Sidmouth itself is peaceful, I have seen barbed wire on the beaches further along the Devon coast, and heard my mother say: 'France has fallen.' We were walking along beside a tall stone wall as she spoke these words, and I imagined it toppling. But how could a *country* fall?

In 1970, I grew my hair into long woolly ringlets again. For when I was six or seven years old I had begged my mother to let me wear my hair in plaits and from then on waged a persistent war against its nature. At school when my friends wanted to tease me they said it was frizzy, negroid, jewish, as if I were not quite like the rest of them— different. When I grew older it was cut short (the urchin cut), when I became sophisticated I lacquered it into a beehive, the fringe flattened against my forehead each night with sellotape. I had it professionally straightened. ('Don't comb it,' said the hairdresser, 'it might fall out.') I ironed it to keep it straight. I had it cropped to the bone.

13

The period of my short cropped hair was also a period when I used to frequent the pubs and clubs of the 'straight gay' scene. In male bars I'd sometimes be mistaken for a boy. I discovered that the way a man eyes up another man is different from the way a man looks at a woman. What if I'd responded to these invitations? Would I have become some Rosalind or Viola of the bars, a Shakespearian master-mistress of someone's passion? But if the camp masquerade of gender was brittle, it was also a half-conscious form of protest against conventional gender roles. When a Hastings publican asked me the–literally–unanswerable question: 'Are you eighteen, young man?', conventions and rules were revealed as absurd, and even reality a farce.

By the time I grew my hair long, hippy men had ringlets too, so I was still androgyne, and the drivers of some of the cars that purred to a halt beside me as I walked along the King's Road were not looking for someone who was all woman. Feminists started to cut off their hair and asked me why I kept mine long. For them long hair–those straight curtains that reached the rim of a mini-dress–meant all the wrong sorts of femininity. But for me long hair symbolised spontaneity and liberation.

*

I was always mad about style. The emphasis at home was on duty. My mother's misfortunes were symbolised, for a time, by her mourning after my grandfather died. Because clothes were rationed, she could obtain only ex-service uniforms 'off coupons'. She had these heavy, unfashionable garments dyed black, and, since it was no longer customary for the bereaved to wear full mourning, she looked almost as bizarre as she would have done dressed in sackcloth and ashes, especially at functions at my school, where the other mothers were wearing the New Look–the new long, full skirts and rounded shoulders. My mother's square, black greatcoat presented an embarrassing contrast to their femininity.

14

The ambiguity of style is that it can be simultaneously display and screen. At parties in the sixties I used to wear a striped trouser suit and a huge-brimmed yellow Biba hat. My appearance during this, my smart phase, seemed both to attract and repel. Once, at a literary party, the plainly-dressed wife of a celebrity berated me angrily for my chic. At a lesbian club I was swept onto the floor by another total stranger. She snatched the cigarette from my mouth and ground it into the floor: 'I nevaire dance weez a woman 'oo smoke.' I disdained these 'uncool' strangers. My purpose was not encounter, but display. I was posed and doll-like as the models Twiggy and Grace Coddington with their Pierrot make-up and Petrouschka limbs. Both trendy dolly and pretty boy, I played out the sexual ambiguity of the mid-sixties.

It was a regression from the fifties, when some of the fashion roles available had had overtones at least of commitment or, if not that, then affirmation of a class position. You could look 'county' or you could look 'tarty', you could also look 'arty' in a Dorelia dirndl skirt, worn with a large man's sweater in a dingy colour, with strings of beads, pre-Raphaelite hair, ballerina shoes and thick, coloured or black stockings. I wore my grandmother's black lisle ones. So, ironically, the mourning clothes that had once so much embarrassed me themselves became part of an existentialist style, a style later to be associated with beatniks, CND and rebellion.

In the sixties the aim was no longer to make a social statement, but to fuse, narcissistically, the glamour of the sexual object with the glamour of the sexual predator. But ambiguity and confusion hid behind this blank-eyed sexual pose.

*

In an endless adolescence I sought to become real by transforming my fleeting and uncouth image in the glass into something more permanent, frozen forever in the beauty of a pose. One day the mirror would give me back myself, but until that time I could not be said fully to exist.

I haunted Harrods, wandering there for hours. I was simply a gaze, I saw without impinging, like a ghost or a soul–a 'personality'–in search of a body to inhabit. In this endless emptiness of adolescent solitude I was no more than an aspirant to existence.

There was another ghost in Harrods. Una, Lady Troubridge, for many years the companion of Radclyffe Hall, the lesbian novelist, strangely clad in monocle, black man's jacket and pin-stripe trousers, sometimes passed along the aisles (I, at any rate, was convinced it was she). Her clothes, like my mother's mourning, were inappropriate and as such a painful exposure of some part of the self that should have been hidden.

Harrods was an endless empty Heaven, and as boring as Heaven would be, arched empty hall after hall–empty even when it was thronged with ghosts.

I haunted the rose-lit, carpet-padded salons, and hoped that each mirror I glanced at–and I looked in them all–would show me as–myself. But I saw only a grim, plain girl, and refused to recognise her. The ghost in the Emporium was window shopping for that image of the self which she could inhabit and thereby become a real person.

Sometimes a woman passed who might be that self. (All beautiful women looked like ballerinas or Audrey Hepburn, with doe eyes and sloping shoulders and sleek, dark hair.) And others passed who hinted at forbidden worlds. A masculine-looking woman with a shock of grey hair and a silky camel coat advanced along the aisles. In her train were a young woman and two young men. All were the epitome of elegance and that camp defiance, a hint of coarseness curdling the aristocratic disdain. I followed them out into the street, but they were lost to sight in a taxi.

In the women's magazines I read there were 'personality tests'. Each month I turned to the magic page and in

16

answering the questions discovered whether I was out-going, the studious type, mysterious or home-loving. Was my favourite colour green, red, brown? Did I like flowery scents, or spicy, or sweet ones? (If I liked them all, was I mad, with some disease of a multiple personality?) The negative of what *Vogue* presented glamorously as the *sportive,* the internationally elegant or the discreetly sexy appeared in less assured magazines as–when you came down to it–the suburban (domestic), sexy (vulgar), intel-lectual (intense) or hearty (butch). In the magazines particularly for teenage girls, the personality quiz held covert messages about etiquette and proper behaviour.

But I believed that if I answered these tests accurately enough I would really become or discover myself. In particular, what colours should I wear to 'express' my 'personality'? Later, my belief in the significance of the sign language of colour was reinforced when a friend gave me a book by Oswald Spengler to read. *The Decline of the West* lifted the test of personality-according-to-colour-preference into the realm of Art:

> Yellow and red are the *popular* colours, the colours of the crowd, of children, of women and of savages. Amongst the Venetians and the Spaniards high per-sonages affected a splendid black or blue, with an unconscious sense of the aloofness inherent in these colours ...
>
> Violet, a red succumbing to blue, is the colour of women no longer fruitful and of priests living in celibacy ...
>
> The brown of Rembrandt ... opened a prospect into an infinity of pure forms ... and thus was attained the inwardness ... which Apollonian man had sought with his strictly somatic art to keep at bay ... Brown thus became the characteristic colour of the soul ... [1]

So the wearing of black, brown and dark blue was to

express my longing to be above the crowd, to devote myself to Art and learning.

There was a definite yet vague excitement in opening a fashion magazine. Their glossy promise drew me irresistibly. Just as pornography arouses the reader to sexual excitement, so these magazines aroused a narcissistic desire. There was the lift of excitement, the distinct erotic thrill in opening the pages, in handling the shiny paper and feasting on the photographs and drawings, so richly extravagant in their devotion to style, of elongated women with jutting hip bones and proudly averted faces. Yet they never fully satisfied the desire they aroused. There was always some obscure disappointment by the time I had hunted through and over every page and licked out the last vestige of content. It was the pornography of narcissism, a form of desire for which there exists no relief.

They exhausted me because the desire I failed to satisfy was so complicated. The fashion magazines promised me the 'dream of identity'. Simultaneously I was truly to *be* myself and *be* the beautiful women at whom I gazed. And then, the magic of fashion offered the absolute in that I myself *became* the perfect, frozen moment of fashion and beauty—no more *anomie* or nausea of the physical and material, for in fashion the body became abstract, it vanished, and in its place stood an essence of oneself simultaneously rigged out as a woman of the world. These fashion magazines were full of a form of magical thinking in which to name something was to conjure it up. They stamped the confusing mass of sensations, limbs, perceptions, moods and viscera that I called 'me' into a sharply outlined mould labelled 'gamine' or 'avant garde student'.

*

But this was not the beginning. By the time I was old enough to read fashion magazines I was already an old hand at investing my own clothes with a mysterious power. They had their own hierarchy. There was always

18

my favourite dress, my favourite colour. I never wanted to be a tomboy, but liked being dolled up. And for my mother too colours were every bit as significant as they were for Oswald Spengler. Red (my favourite colour when I was Chatterbox) was forbidden me, for as a blonde I had to wear the hated blue. My grandmother might wear pink and brown, since she had dark hair, although for her as an older woman red would have been as unsuitable as it was for the fair-haired. Green was unlucky, purple unheard of and yellow 'difficult'. Black of course represented grief, yet, as with the black stockings, it had a double nature. I was once given a black velvet dress with a lace collar, and this lifted me to the height of sophistication, so that sophistication itself came to seem like a way of breaking rules. If you were really chic you could transform black from the mutilation of mourning into the ultimate in allure.

Then there were clothes prescribed for each section of the day. There were my mother's 'coats and skirts' for luncheon at Fullers or the Cadena café in the Arcade. There was the afternoon frock she wore when she took me to parties. There were cocktail frocks, dinner gowns and full evening dress. Women in trousers were an abomination according to my grandfather (as were women who 'painted their faces') and 'slacks' (later 'drainpipes') were for the most informal occasions only. Tweeds and brown leather were for the country, barathea and black patent leather only for town wear. To find yourself wearing a pair of black 'court' shoes in a country lane would be to let the Absolute leak away. To stick to these strict rules was a symbolic reassurance. A correct outward appearance meant that inwardly one was 'all right'.

All this had nothing to do with sexuality, although the erotic purpose of dress was always disturbingly, latently there. It had more to do with good taste and ladylike middle-classness. So here was another contradiction of

19

fashion. It represented conformity and individualism simultaneously, since clothes were also to express self. In clothes the elusive, fluid and, it sometimes seemed, non-existent 'personality' revealed itself and was expressed. The fashion magazines admonished me to 'be myself'. 'Clothes should reveal, not conceal your personality.' But where and what was my personality?

My 'figure' was certainly not the right shape, but I never really thought of myself as a body. My body in itself was not important. It was simply a piece of raw material and a hindrance in its reluctance to be metamorphosed into a fashion image. So, although the explicit philosophy of the magazines was that fashion was an unveiling of the self, a backdrop against which the drama that was one's person-ality was to play itself out, the process they described was the *creation* of personality. There was no essential inner self that expressed itself in appearance. Appearance *was* essence. Your inmost self was the frozen, perfect, outward display. This display transformed personality from drama into tableau, translated you into the realm of the Absolute, and conquered the mess, the flux and flow of life, banishing the creased skirt, twisted stockings and greasy nose.

In order to achieve this perfection it was necessary to conform to rules that went far beyond convention and reached the condition of a way of life and even the discipline of a religious order. Just as the nun by way of her adherence to the rituals of prayer, work, worship, fasting and meditation entered–it was said–a world of freedom, so I, if my observances of the rituals of fashion were pious enough, would myself experience the joy of the faithful. The nun was to be spiritually united with God. I was to be united with myself.

So one could travel from the pornography of narcissism to the religion of narcissism. And it became clear that narcissism was not selfishness, egocentricity or self love. Rather, it was an arduous perfectionism, and entailed the conquering of the material world in pursuit of the purity of ideas.

*

In some of the books I read fashion was linked to a whole 'art of living' (very much a phrase of the early fifties) and with a fashionable world that fused art, chic and a romantic realm of forbidden love. This was the world of Proust and Diaghilev at one level, of Cecil Beaton at another. Through the stories of Colette, the memoirs of Misia Sert, through biographies and autobiographies, I entered this realm of passion and self expression.

In these books, life became a work of art, love a perpetual high. Every banquet or dinner party was a still life by a Post Impressionist, and the coarsest liaison became an operatic aria, while to see a great painting or listen to a quartet became an experience that transcended life itself. I failed to notice how tragic was Misia Sert's life—hideous deaths and dreadful betrayals are found in every chapter of her book, which I read simply as an Arabian Night's tale of luxury and glamour. If only I could have lived in that world! My fashion bible was Cecil Beaton's *The Glass of Fashion* which contained a wealth of descriptions of 'ladies of fashion'—an embarrassingly wide variety of patterns for me to model myself on. Again I failed to notice how many of them died early or tragically, how many were childless, lost husbands, lovers and huge fortunes along the way. I read avidly of these women I had never heard of:

> As fantastic as any character in romantic literature, Mrs Rita de Acosta Lydig graced the opening cycles of the twentieth century with a perfectionism that would have been rare in any period since the Renaissance. A woman of unusual intensity, she lived up to the extraordinarily high standards and ideals that she had set for herself, paying dearly in that most difficult of all causes—to make oneself a work of art.

21

Or there was Phillis de Janzé:

> To see Phillis de Janzé turn her head, laugh and swing
> her dangling earrings from side to side was to marvel at
> a complete work of art. She could have been produced
> only in a period of the highest civilisation.
>
> But nature alone had not created this phenomenon.
> Phillis, as a result of her artistry had helped to make
> her own appearance the tour de force that it became,
> though as soon as she had finished the creation she
> forgot about it . . . She lived by and for her amours . . .
>
> She was wonderfully oblivious to the squalors and
> mediocrities of life . . . To see her shopping at Fortnum
> and Mason with her maid, friend and companion, both
> wearing identical hats, was like coming across a figure
> out of mythology, a goddess living in disguise, or a
> supernatural spirit with her Pekingese dog as her
> familiar.

The dedication of these exotic ladies dazzled me. There
seemed to be no lengths to which they would not go to
express this essence of fashion and chic I found so elusive.
One was in the habit of 'leaving the room for a moment to
have a Vitamin B$_1$ injection and [would] then return
nonchalantly a moment later, taking up the conversation
where she left off'. Another nearly suffered martyrdom in
the cause of chic when her costume for a fancy dress ball
went wrong:

> At the moment of being plugged in a disaster took
> place: the costume was short-circuited and, instead of
> being lighted up with a thousand stars, the Marquesa
> suffered an electric shock that sent her into a back-
> ward somersault. She did not recover in time to
> attend the party, leaving a note that stated simply
> *'Mille regrets'*.[2]

So there could be something almost heroic in one's

dedication to fashion, which might, it appeared, require one to risk one's life, as well as to court mysterious illnesses, bankruptcy and morphine addiction.

I took it all in earnest. Desperately serious, I drank in the snobbery, the chic, and the strange mixture of simplicity (Garbo and Chanel) and exotic originality that seemed to be required if I was indeed to become a work of art.

*

During those years I sometimes sat in front of my stepmother's bedroom mirror which, like a triptych, had three sections, a central glass and two wings hinged to the sides. If I arranged these at the correct angle I could see the back of my head. Behind my head I could also see the infinite regress–the angle and the image of myself in '*profil perdu*', repeated over and over again, rushing back into infinity. It was like looking down an endless empty corridor into eternity.

Three

Multiple reflections of self shared my inner world with romantic images of the Other. In my daydreams school prefects, film stars and tennis players in turn filled the role of romantic rescuer who was to swoop down and lift me to a heavenly realm of love. Outwardly, my end of term reports suggested, I was a wooden and non-committal schoolgirl, whose work often disappointed my teachers. They believed I was lazy. In fact I was often depressed, and when not depressed I seethed with unfulfilled passions. If I seemed bored or absent-minded in the classroom, this was only because I was watching the cinema screen in my head. The images that flickered across it showed me as a kept woman in the Paris of 1900 or an aristocratic heroine in eighteenth-century France. My knowledge of erotic love was gleaned from the novels of Colette and Proust, from the serialisation of *Forever Amber*–a mildly salacious bestseller of the period–in the *Sunday Dispatch*, and from the romantic adventures of the Scarlet Pimpernel as described by Baroness Orczy. Her absurdly innocent novels attracted me because the hero–actually a daring infiltrator who snatches innocent French aristocrats from the jaws of the guillotine and the revolutionary terror–is forced to present himself as ineffectual fop, deceiving even his wife, whom he ardently loves, but who for long scorns him as an effeminate idiot–another instance of disguise, and of hidden identities. (But in my fantasy life, I was always the Scarlet Pimpernel myself, as well as his adored wife.) The raw, dusty atmosphere of school was simply an irrelevance.

The school building itself symbolised the disjointed

relationship between daily life and secret dreams. The façade, of red brick crowned with a Dutch gable of white stone, the entrance hall, tiled in black and white marble and the panelled hall with its gallery and large studio windows, were gracious and elegant. We schoolgirls, however, never mounted the front steps, but clattered down into the basement, a dark and noisy underworld. There we lurked and dawdled in the locker rooms with their dim electric lighting, their splintered floors and scratched locker doors. We banged in and out of the lavatories with their noisy iron bolts. We hung about the corridor that led to the kitchens and dining rooms and eventually led you round a corner to the gym. Food trolleys rattled up and down the metal strips set into the red tiled floor making a noise like shunting engines. These trolleys carried a sordid load of sticky, grey suet puddings, gelatinous stews, cakes that stuck to the roof of the mouth and were served with a watered down marmalade sauce that resembled brilliantine, fish in slimy batter, and beetroots in a slimy white sauce which they bled into, turning it a horrid pink. At the end of each dinner they returned to the kitchens piled with an even more sordid debris of greasy plates, trays of fat and scraps, and cold roast potatoes, hard as stones.

This nether region, ministering to the body, seemed debased and somehow furtive. From it we sprang up the stone stairs to an airy world of learning and the mind.

But was it? What they taught us interested me, but the model of learned womanhood presented by our teachers left me ambivalent.

This was a transition period in women's education. The portrait of Dame Ethel Strudwyck, the headmistress who had just retired, gleamed down on us as we gathered in the hall for prayers each morning. I had an impression of her, even then, as a pioneer campaigner for women's education, a feminist in other words, though that word was not in fact used. Formidable, genial, perhaps in her own way worldly,

25

she might have had something in common with those women heads of religious orders in pre-Reformation England who ran great abbeys and nunneries. An eleven-year-old in the lowest form, I arrived just as she was leaving, but although I never spoke to her I have a clear memory of her as an awesomely elevated yet good humoured, rather masculine presence, her hair folded back from her face in two wings, her chin folding into her collar as she stared down over her glasses and showed her large teeth in a smile, her whole manner suggesting a relaxed confidence some of her fellow teachers lacked.

Many of the teachers came from the same pre-war generation of educated women who had probably been at least influenced by feminism. Now their day was passing. New conservative attitudes towards women were in the ascendancy and these were to be given dramatic voice on my first Speech Day, when, as was customary, a member of the Board of Governors addressed the assembled school and parents. On this occasion the Governor who stood up to speak was a smooth, rather young and good-looking man. He smiled disarmingly and proceeded to utter dreadful heresies, under the guise of being modern. Girls, he said, should be educated to be wives. He developed this theme with sophistication. By implication at least the old ideas of equality and equal education for women were fusty and prudish. Gasps and giggles from the audience punctuated his speech. Afterwards my mother was furious. The speech was reported on the front page of the *Daily Telegraph*. It was almost a minor scandal, for he'd somehow hinted that girls should be glamorous, desirable. I thought it was rather wonderful. Didn't I long for glamour, after all?

About three years later a well-known journalist wrote an article in a Sunday newspaper in which she criticised the education of grammar school girls on the grounds that they were taught only useless subjects, such as Greek and Latin, while the useful skills of cooking and sewing were neglected–more of the new conservatism, dressed up as progressive and as a 'realistic' approach. I did think that was rather silly, since cooking was so much easier than Latin and was a skill that could be quickly acquired as the need arose. My Latin teacher, angry, told me: 'She was at this school herself, you know.' I guessed that she felt betrayed.

The trouble was, though, that to our cruel, caricaturing, schoolgirl eyes, many of our teachers did seem rather dowdy, and, in the case of those–the majority–who were unmarried, we were unable to imagine their lives as other than two-dimensional and emotionally impoverished. What life seemed like to them, how they experienced it, we had no idea. There was a rigid barrier between them and us. We all met only on the dusty, barren plains of a learning from which much of the feeling had been drained. They presented themselves to us as shy, dry spinsters. No doubt to them we were superficial, lumpish and insensitive, and, to make matters worse, in many cases, with the superior airs bestowed by wealth and family confidence.

There was, it is true, so far as I was concerned, an absolute thrill in turning out an accurate, even conceivably an elegant Latin translation, or in unravelling some piece of history. But when it came to literature, although I could wallow in Keats's melancholy or in Wordsworth's oneness with nature, I could never get a full sense of why *they* enthused. That they–the school mistresses–had feelings too seemed almost immodest. Occasionally they gave you little glimpses of their lives, but these glimpses too were puzzling. One of them spoke one day of 'the happiest, loveliest day of my life' when she stood on the Acropolis in Athens, and it seemed sad to me–perhaps I misunderstood her–to have had one day in your life that stood out as so noticeably more happy than the rest. Another, in a rather different vein, recommended the long eighteenth-century novel *Clarissa Harlowe* on the grounds that it was the best novel in the world to read on a winter afternoon while lying on the sofa in front of the fire and eating your way through a box of chocolates, and the self indulgence of this statement shocked me.

A few of them got married, and this shocked me too, naively priggish as I was. I could not imagine why women in their thirties would get married. It was surely something you did when young, or not at all.

There was a telling contrast between the teachers and some of the mothers who wafted elegantly in for end of term concerts and plays and for the Speech Day at the end of each year. They were certainly glamorous, even if they seemed a little bored and weary in their furs and silky dresses. At their sides there often stood a father, encased in the costliest of city overcoats, with pinkly scrubbed face and a special adult smile. Those adult smiles with their undertones of–sexuality? cynicism? weariness? self satisfaction?–were certainly not to be found on the faces of our teachers, nor for that matter on my mother's face. I connected those smiles with wealth and worldliness, with a world of sophistication to which I wanted to belong.

Despite the lack of glamour associated with female learning, it must have been at school that I first learned to think of myself as an intellectual and first assumed the word as an identity. Although the teachers might often seem dull, although they did not say why they had chosen to teach a particular subject or what they liked about it, (taking enthusiasm perhaps too much for granted, just as we took our privilege too much as a matter of course) they must have communicated some enthusiasm to some of us sometimes. And anyway I had always liked lessons and reading because it was there that I shone. Learning the answers quick as a flash, playing with thoughts, stringing words together–it was like a little tap dance in the mind, clackety-clack with the nimble footwork, the tossing curls and the bright smile. Showing off!–it was a reincarnation of Chatterbox.

The identity 'intellectual', though, was more than performance–it was a persona. I devoured books because they opened gates to a secret, imaginary life of emotion and eroticism. At the same time to 'go to university' was a calling in itself (beyond which I did not look) and gave life an outward purpose. Perhaps the identity was constructed not–wanly–from what I saw of my teachers, but from what I began to understand about the parents of some of my fellow pupils. Hitherto I'd had a restricted idea of the kinds of work it was possible to do in adult life. I knew only of doctors, colonels and lawyers. One of my friends longed to be a nurse, while my mother urged me to become a 'civil servant'–whatever that was. The parents of some of my friends at school, on the other hand, did all sorts of creative things. There were psychotherapists, writers and ballet dancers, there were musicians, historians, people who worked for the BBC, and even MPs. And their homes seemed to me wonderful places where art, creativity and things of the mind were endlessly discussed. I stood with my nose pressed to the pane of this wonderful world, and stared at the delectable display of melt-in-the-mouth marvels of the mind on display like so many rows of patisseries, cakes and biscuits.

Something else–I began to notice that there were those in this milieu who did not vote Tory. At first, when the gossip went round that a few of our teachers voted Labour, I was surprised. It seemed eccentric. They were on the losing side anyway, for it was the 1951 general election, at which the Conservative Party was returned to power. This was the occasion for another trip to Harrods, for my father took me to watch the election results on a specially constructed board erected in the banking hall. A red or blue electric light flashed the announcement of each result. A small crowd had gathered to watch. The men leaned on their umbrellas, the women were poised on high heels. A discreet cheer went up each time another blue light

29

flashed. There was an air of polite jubilation.

Then I discovered that the parents of some of my friends, like my teachers, voted Labour. This could not be dismissed as dusty eccentricity. I began to associate 'socialism' with the slightly bohemian (or so it seemed to me then) intellectual life of these families, who all seemed to live–or seem in my memory to have lived–in elegantly untidy little Georgian houses in the backwaters of Hammersmith, Chelsea and Kensington.

I was solemnly obsessed with art and music. Pained by the commercialised vulgarity of advertising and pop, I yearned for a better society in which there would be no place for the sentimentality of Donald Peers (a popular singer) or the hateful brashness of *Oklahoma,* for suburban sprawl and the stupidities of television. Like my grandmother, I looked down my long nose at it all, culturally snobbish for the sincerest reasons.

I was also terrified by the nuclear menace, that dark blight that hung over us. One day I chanced upon a copy of the *New Statesman* in the local library. Its front page carried an article about the Farnborough air display, arguing that the armaments industry was to blame for the proliferation of weapons, even for the nuclear threat itself.

So that was it! Money and profit were at the root of it all, just as they were at the root of vulgar advertising and cheap music. So cultural snobbery and moral revulsion began to be transformed into an abstract socialism. I began to perceive capitalism as the modern source of injustice, ugliness and poverty, while tempted to reject industrialism itself.

My political beliefs, such as they were, had not yet become part of any identity. Still, it began to seem rather old-fashioned to be such a dyed-in-the-wool Tory. The civilised tolerance of the parents of some of my friends edged in some cases into social concern and social conscience, even into political commitment. A fellow pupil explained to me that food rationing had been a good thing (at home we saw it as an oppressive deprivation of human freedom) since it equalised the distribution of food and was therefore fairer. This was a new thought to me. Although I believed *we* were poor, I had no notion of the poverty that meant going hungry and cold. I only felt sorry for myself because we had dingy decorations and no telephone or fitted carpets.

I began to subject the Tory philosophy to a new and hostile examination. What *did* it amount to after all but moral philistinism? The Tories supported hanging and flogging and were all for nuclear bombs. More to the point, I began to meet a few 'sub debs' and their escorts, many of whom were Young Conservatives, and I thought they were terrible. Sub debs were young women hanging about in Earls Court and Kensington who were not presented officially at Court to the Queen, but who were living out a pale reflection of 'the Season' at a few dismal parties. The Young Conservatives, youth branch of the Tory Party, was probably the most flourishing British youth organisation at the time. But I found the Kensington bed sitters, the young hearties and the limp taffeta infinitely depressing. To become a left-wing intellectual was the swiftest exit route from that particularly chilling scene. I took it.

Four

With a schoolfriend I enrolled for a summer course at a French university. At last I was to go Abroad. At St Malo we leant over the fortifications and watched the waves breaking against rocks. So cold and grey off the South coast of England, here the sea had a greenish-blue depth. We sat in a café on the square. The thick coffee cups and the strange oblong bricks of sugar were foreign. Everything here would be different.

But I was to be disappointed. We stayed in a teachers' training college, a large, square, grey building situated in flat, uninspiring country near La Rochelle. The landscape was no different from an English one, nor was the weather better than at home. I'd expected an atmosphere of dreamlike brightness. Walking through an Impressionist painting, I too would be changed.

On the contrary, I was trapped in my Englishness. The students, from all over Europe, seemed compelled to live out national stereotypes, and sexual identity was fixed within these caricatures. There were sultry Italian girls. One evening one of these gave an impromptu performance of the Neapolitan song *Return to Sorrento* which she sang with such lushly kitsch throbbings that she seemed to embody, unselfconsciously, a whole romantic stereotype of the South, rather as those senoritas on cigar boxes do. There were blonde Swedish girls, and sleek, sloe-eyed Spaniards who lay in wait for them like lizards. There were pompous, handsome Germans, the first I'd met.

There was one bearded Englishman who looked as if he'd stepped out of a film about the RAF or safaris in Kenya. But apart from him the British cut a sorry figure in this charade of national character. We were at the bottom of the sexual league table. We moved about in a group, shabby public school boys and earnest young women. We haunted a little night club where I at first drank the green, red and orange *sirops,* but soon discovered Pineau, which was as sickly sweet as the *sirops,* but which, unlike them, made you quickly drunk. I was quietly drunk most evenings, because I was secretly disappointed by France and out of tune with my own stereotypic Englishness.

It was here that I became fully conscious for the first time of how wide a gap existed between 'me' and an imperious identity to which I was expected to conform: the Young Girl. The Young Girl had no past, no sense of guilt, no shame. She was pure surface, inviolable, fresh, free. It did not matter whether she was technically a virgin or not, so long as she appeared as an innocent white page on which each man who saw her longed to write his name. She was not made dusty and smudged, as I was, by the ink off the books she'd read. She did not read. She smiled and frowned decisively. Her words, her gestures, were full of clear cut certainty. Her relationship with the environment was one of unselfconscious mastery. Mine was clumsy and tacky. Young men might have doubts, thoughts, moods. The Young Girl just *was* grace and poise. She was unitary, and unfractured by contradiction or conflict. It was strange, given that woman signified emotion, but she was void of feelings. She carved a path through her social world with wonderful and devastating blankness.

*

Waiting to go to university, I took a job at the local public library. This interlude held me together through a summer of unreality and loneliness. Might I be going mad, body and mind separating and floating off in different directions with no 'identity' to hold them together?

Recovering from a brief illness, I sat in our back yard between cliff-like houses, and read about philosophy and man's cosmic loneliness in the universe. It made me giddy to watch myself dwindling to a speck of dust floating down an infinity without beginning or end. The universe, an enormous yawn, was about to swallow me up.

Then there was Love, which had visited me in a disturbing form. The beginnings of sex, petting at parties, stupidly good-looking boys in darkened cinemas and in the fetishistic, black leather interiors of cabs, those padded cells of sex–what was all that by comparison with *Her*–a woman whose masculinity had excited me because she was a woman. She'd spoken of sexual experience as a pain you wanted to last forever, and now I felt lost without that pain, without the daily shock of her violent male-femaleness. It had been like braving a sea so cold and rough that you had to gasp for breath, winded.

The waves had flung me onto a lonely shore, and left me beached, stranded. Now I was coming round, exhausted. Where was identity in all this? I, who had positively courted femininity and had rejected the drab images of womanhood surrounding me at home and at school, now found the boundary between masculine and feminine blurred. It could no longer be said that I 'felt' feminine or masculine. Sexual feeling seemed to destroy gender identity, and I was just a raging 'I'.

But perhaps I could forget about it. The daily routines of my job at the public library came as a welcome return to some sort of normality.

We juniors gathered at half past eight each morning in the basement staffroom and drank nescafé, except for John who lived in digs and who mixed himself beaten eggs and milk when he arrived and swallowed it down as breakfast. Before the doors opened at nine, Harry and I had already started to order and straighten the shelves. Harry was large and good natured. We exchanged political confidences as we crouched by the shelves. I told him I was an Existential-ist. He confessed he'd been in the Young Communist

League. He good humouredly hated the rich. But before the summer was out he'd left to earn more money as a debt collector: 'I know it's a dead-end job, but I need the lolly.'

Gwyneth's scarlet lipstick framed white teeth. A scarlet ribbon held her pony tail. She wore a scarlet circular skirt and white blouse and cardigan. She was definitely not a Young Girl. She had too much Welsh sharpness and humour for that. Her banter with John and Harry and her telephone conversations with boyfriends hinted at some kind of bitter, black-market bargain that might be made with men. It was clear that for her sex was far from being the passionate fusion of souls I envisaged it to be.

I was later to recognise Harry, Gwyneth and John in the pages of novels by Kingsley Amis and John Wain. Like the Angry Young Men, they disliked authority but had no clear idea how to subvert it other than on a day-to-day level of jokes, mockery and innuendo. All were scared of the chief librarian who scuttled across the marble entrance hall long after the rest of us were at work, looking with his protruding eyes and sideways gait like a huge St Malo lobster in the watery half light.

A small hierarchy of rather worn men and one upholstered woman separated us from him. She had a mother to support, they wives and children. To them my incompetence seemed far more subversive than the faces Harry, Gwyneth and John pulled. Who could believe my incompetence was not an elaborate joke? I was a walking disaster, dropping piles of books, snapping at old age pensioners in the queue to have their books stamped, as I grew flustered under their rheumy, patient stares, going berserk on the switchboard and pulling out all the stops, cutting off the 'Chief' while he was talking to his wife. Harry and Gwyneth giggled, but I was horror-struck.

My stupidity, humiliating to me, seemed to be interpreted as insolence by the deputy librarian. I was called into his office. On my first day he'd benevolently shown me round,

35

expansive on the subject of 'my baby'–a special collection of local history books. Now he snapped: 'You don't care in the least–you're just here until you go to *Oxford*–it doesn't matter to you whether you do the job properly or not–you don't care twopence.' Unfair! I stared woodenly, as tears of embarrassment filled my eyes. My silence and haughty indifference concealed the pain of this unbelievable confrontation.

Was it just that I was always in a dream? Was I listening to those heavy waves on the shore–faraway now? Waiting for madness to descend? The gap between self and identity widened: 'Not to worry,' said kind Harry, 'he's just jealous.' But how could that vinegary persona harbour emotions?

He–and maybe the others, kind though they were–possibly saw me in class terms of which I myself was naively unconscious. My accent and manners, shrilly tinged with upper-middle-classness, formed a part of my identity, but a part I did not 'see'. In Harrods I'd felt an uneasiness because my identity seemed so amorphous, and its boundaries so unclear. Now, I banged up against hard edges of self, as if I were shut up in a darkened room and, in the blackout, knocked against my stupidity, my clumsiness, my class manner with its built-in insensitivity, unfamiliar furniture of that hitherto empty chamber of the self.

*

In the library I did, though, find books that opened up a world more real than the inessential world of the daily, library routine. I read the books in the 'special' section kept behind the counter, those considered to be too sexually explicit or too immoral to be placed on the open shelves. I read *The Well of Loneliness* and *The Second Sex*. I read a novel called *Into The Labyrinth*. It was about an adolescent girl who has a love affair with her father's mistress. The older woman is dominating, powerful, even brutal, yet in the end she marries the father and turns overnight into a model of passive femininity. I found this book disturbing, as I did *The Well of Loneliness,* for each presented me with a choice only between a mutilated masculinity for which I felt revulsion and a femininity I equally rejected. Each of the 'powerful women' in these books, too, the mistress, and the 'heroine' of *The Well of Loneliness,* Stephen, appeared to me to betray my romantic vision of lesbianism. And although I passionately identified with Simone de Beauvoir's feminism, she too was ambiguous about lesbians: 'They live like men in a world without men'–was it really like that? She also could not allay my anxieties or even answer my questions about my sexuality. But one day the title of a book that *was* housed on the open shelves–presumably because it was considered too literary and obscure to endanger the morals of the old ladies and unemployed men who moped about the library–caught my eye: *Cities of the Plain* by Marcel Proust. Surreptitiously I began to read, and read, at intervals, all day, within the square bastion of the counter. I was enthralled because I'd found a world in which sexuality, glamour, vice and moral grandeur were wonderfully locked together within the embrace of Art, in this novel, twelve volumes of it, expounding an aesthetic philosophy that made sense of my madness and confusion. Here was a writer who linked for me two things that had been separated–the possibilities of sensual pleasure and the world of intellect and art.

Proust opened up whole vistas of identity. Here were men and women related in a social world which suggested that behind every appearance was a different reality, that behind each of the personas we present to the world is a whole series of identities and disguises. Here is a young and loving mistress metamorphosed into a consummate whore, into a worldly salon hostess ... she is also a lesbian posed in boy's clothes for a painter of genius who dies in obscurity, leaving his works with their beauty unrecognised and also, so to speak, in disguise.

37

Proust described a world in which not only were the humble daily gestures–of making a telephone call, or eating a sponge cake–invested with the glamour of an aesthetic meaning, but one in which also formless desires and dire longings were both named and justified. All desire, it seemed, however damned, had its own romance and beauty, and its own symbolism. Art redeemed ugliness.

*

The glittering, snaky, sinister 'lesbian' cut through my confusions at the age of eighteen. If I was *that,* then I could wash my hands of social success or failure. My general incompetence would dwindle to insignificance. By declaring myself unacceptable I forestalled all possible forms of rejection.

So it was clutching the lifebelt of 'lesbian' to my chest that I was launched, without having been taught how to swim, into a sea of social contradictions, Oxford under-graduate life in 1955. When I now look back down the telescope at that high-pitched world, I catch a glimpse of 'myself'. At the time I felt both amorphous and wooden.

Woodenness might be mistaken for what is strangely known as 'self possession' or *sang froid*–cold blood. On arrival–as I later discovered–my friend Jenny and I were christened Glynis Johns and Diana Dors–stepping in high heels like a pair of J. Arthur Rank starlets out of a taxi, turning, so young and so glacial, to face our gothic hall of residence.

In London I'd touched on the outer fringes of bohemian life. A childhood friend–the little boy with whom I'd charged through the Park brandishing my sword, and who'd now become a jazz-crazy curate–had taken me to a club where they played 'trad'. I'd felt at home in the smoky darkness. I'd liked the hoarse singers in a beam of light. I'd been anonymous and normal among the women with pony tails and dirndl skirts. The men wore tweed jackets and polonecks. These were the sorts of places Gwyneth and

Harry would frequent. Afterwards we'd sat in Soho coffee bars, and I'd looked about me in the vain hope of seeing someone smoking a 'reefer' or Proustian lesbians hunched in corners.

There were many Oxfords, but none was a bohemia. To me Oxford seemed at the beginning bourgeois, smart, snobbish. Pleasure was a timetable, of champagne parties at noon, tea parties at four and sherry parties at six. An almost Victorian art of sedate flirtation must have developed in the artificial atmosphere of–especially–the teas, as the muffins, walnut cake, and toast with quince conserve or Gentlemen's Relish were passed and the Earl Grey tea was poured. I had no flow of high spirits. Unnerved, I froze– cold blood that meant a stupid silence while the Young Girls chattered and smiled. Even after I'd learnt to imitate their brightness, I still felt mine was a frozen glitter, too hard, too sharp, too bitter, or a wooden wit, clumsy and crude.

The narrow, though brightly lit segment of Oxford that I knew, which was only one of several undergraduate Oxfords, offered a social life both fevered and regimented, an atmosphere of mannered sophistication mixed with arrogant innocence. I'd expected that Oxford would be the opening out of adult life, but it was the last children's tea party. We could lead the life of bright young things for a few years, before stepping out into 1960 to become– ordinary. That may have been the reason for the feverish flush, the champagne-fizz bubbles of anxiety breaking against the rim of one's consciousness, the relentless brightness. And our social rituals were gestures to ward off the middle-classness that awaited us after we'd finished with this hysterical round of 'fun'.

In the midst of this gaiety I was hysterical too–and at the same time distanced, wary, different. I was aware of myself as separated from this upper bourgeoisie. In a sense I lacked a father. My parents were divorced, my father was retired

39

and his colonial past anomalous, not smart. That I came from an impoverished background caused dissonance and unease.

My friendship with Barbara might bridge the gap between self and social identity. Barbara was the same age as I was but much more knowing. She was tiny and vivacious, with blazing red hair, dead white skin and pale green eyes, her porcelain make up was in place before breakfast and she dressed formally, stalking the corridors in high heels and straight skirts while the rest of us slopped about in our jeans or our tartan drainpipes and our ballerina flatties. Her slightly bent, purposeful gait bore witness to a certain determination in her character, and, without knowing whether I liked her or not, I let myself be swept up in her sophistication. My identity seemed amorphous and uncertain beside her crisply frilled one. I envied her certainty and ruthlessness. Like everyone else, Barbara discussed Life late into the night, punctuating her serious talk with a cry of: 'Do you see *at all* what I mean?' But at the same time she reconstituted life's serious affairs into a stream of hilarious episodes. Identity became once more a matter of poise, pose and style, and I, uneasily torn between moral purpose and glamour, admired her singled-minded pursuit of the smart. (Who would have guessed that she'd marry an ardently Christian doctor, and find her way with him to relief work in Latin America–strange transformation of identity?)

To begin with we both lived in a hall of residence run by nuns. Sensible and down to earth, they did not interfere in our lives, but Barbara soon left the poky, many-cornered rooms, the dark-varnished pine and the twisted corridors for digs in an eighteenth-century house filled with pretty, shabby furniture and old books. I stayed, envious, in my turret room, which I attempted to glamorise with Gauguin prints, a shelf-full of the right paperbacks and an African counterpane (at least that part of my background had begun to seem exotic).

40

I was not unreflectively, triumphantly part of a class, in the way that Barbara and her friends were or seemed to be. Behind me always lurked shabbiness. They lived in houses where comfort shielded you amongst soft carpets, polished floors and furniture melting with age and value. There, there were pleasures for every mood. There were swimming pools, travel abroad, and meals in smart restaurants. There were débutante dances, country weekends, first nights, and the satisfying clunk of names being dropped. There were first editions, Morris wallpapers, private dressmakers and cakes from Fortnum and Mason. All were proffered politely, with smiles of complicity and complacency, as if these privileges were both natural and a reward for virtue. The pleasures of this life were accepted calmly, as necessities.

A strident display of emotion would have jarred, or so I felt, in these softly-lit rooms. Or rather, there was always the danger of appearing vulgar. There was always the danger that a gesture, a vowel, would betray you as– horribly–a stray from some inferior class. Passion and vulgarity, though, became acceptable and even desirable once transformed into some theatricality or drama. You could be an Anglo-Catholic or an atheist, a homosexual or an adulteress, a diplomat or a spy, a crossings sweeper or a criminal, provided that it could be made amusing. As masks, such identities were entertaining. Genuine commitment was a tomb.

Barbara and I could both be rather heartless. Like my grandfather, who had collected butterflies, we chloroformed the bright moment and pinned it, fading, to a piece of cork. Drunk with words and fascinated by their sharpness, dazzled by the power to make others laugh, we jazzed up the truth and caricatured anyone we could lay our hands on.

Barbara represented to me a myth of Oxford that I believed in–that the privileged *were* special. At the same

41

time I partly hated the smartness. I developed a sly, bitter cynicism, took up a blasé pose, refused to succumb to the fashionable enthusiasms–for *The Lord of the Rings,* for *Look Back in Anger*–my failure to please and my hurt at rejection curdling into an inability to conform in any circumstances, a compulsion to reject what Barbara's friends decreed wonderful. I judged them snobs from the confines of my own special snobbery, the snobbery of nihilism.

*

There was also romantic Oxford. Oxford idealised itself. In some benighted hinterland stood the Cowley motor works, but I lived in the 'real' Oxford elevated far above the industrial estates and the slums of St Ebbe's. Like a Renaissance engraving, Oxford floated on a cloud of its own eternal realness, a sort of paradisal city above the grime, decay and earthly cares of the industrial world.

This was the city of learning. It was in this world that I sat in the old libraries. Despite the American tourists who clustered in the courtyard each summer, the library known as Duke Humphries was a private place–medieval. There, seated at a high ledge of warped wood I stared at the bank of ancient, leather, gilt-lettered tomes, a wall of impenetrable learning, all Latin and law, of an obscurity so profound that I too dwindled to utter insignificance. It was with relief that I was relieved of my identity in the twilight of the Tudor hall. These were my happiest hours, when, thankfully anonymous I could lose myself in medieval literature. As I read I visualised a procession, as brightly illuminated as the manuscripts over which my neighbours pored, of medieval saints and sinners, fine fellows and earthy wives, delicate nuns and envious clerks, men and women of substance and those who lived on their wits–characters who could be classified according to the medieval scheme, as sanguine, phlegmatic, choleric or melancholic, according to the balance of 'humours' in each, their

42

temperaments related to the elements, to earth, air, fire and water, which in turn were related to astral influences and the signs of the Zodiac.

Oxford was romantic in a way that suited middle-class adolescence. A pre-Raphaelite medievalism tinged our lives. Brigitte Bardot movies might be shown at the cinemas, and GIs from the American base might be seen in the town, but we lived in a Tennysonian dream. You could take a bus and then walk out into the cold spring countryside, gaze at the Cotswold hills and at the black hatching of branches against a white sky, pick primroses, explore the graveyards of the old wool towns, where the mossy tombstones were carved like bales of fleece–all this beautiful *because* of the poetry that could be quoted, *because* of the return past the suburban houses and Cooper's marmalade factory into the blue evening and the traffic at the roundabout. There was North Oxford when the lilac and laburnum dropped in the languor of an unexpected heatwave, the scent of wallflowers so thick you had to swim through it to reach the depths of a weed-tangled river fit for a Victorian Ophelia. There was the dim purple mist round grey spires and autumn trees, and rusty chestnuts dripping with melancholy over Christ Church meadow. This was a form of romanticism that confounded nature with emotion. Oxford reeked of the pathetic fallacy.

There was a jarring disjuncture between this romantic Oxford and the Oxford that was Barbara's world. Romantic Oxford was preoccupied with a personal world of sincerity and feeling and approached these matters with the Victorian earnestness that seemed so much part of the mist, the dim buildings and the cosy fireside teas. Those dreamy after-noons in the firelight, intense discussions of philosophy and art with a young man who wanted to kiss you but who lacked the vulgarity to grab you on his faded college sofa, this was an Oxford in which we aspired to *rightness* in life.

Aspiration mingled awkwardly with desire on the sofa, especially for young women–Young Girls. What was expected of us? A man could express his earnestness of purpose in scholarship or religion. Worldly male Barbaras could pursue ambition in the smart political and theatrical worlds of undergraduate Oxford. But a woman somehow had to be everything, if she was to make her mark at all. Each women's college, it is true, had its own style, its own caricature of an identity. St Hilda's signified social success, St Hugh's was all about hockey and a grim kind of swotting, Lady Margaret Hall was socially correct, Somerville represented true scholarship. St Anne's, my own college, was the college of the well-adjusted. Our Principal told us we were being educated to become diplomats' wives.

Marriage! I was astonished, discussing Henry James's *The Portrait of a Lady* with a friend of Barbara's, to discover that this young woman had taken the novel as a paradigm for her own life and had totally identified with the heroine. A wrong choice of suitor from amongst those who happened to present themselves would be as fateful for her as it had been for Isabel Archer. Yet we did not talk often or much about marriage. Undergraduate life was a life of seeming freedom and aimlessness, and romantic Oxford seemed less concerned with social institutions than with the development of private spheres of feeling and with a personal response to life, expressed perhaps in religious sentiment, artistic sensibility or in a romantic love that had little to do with legal contract. There might be conflict between personal relationships and work, but that was a conflict within the boundaries of the rightness to which so many aspired. It affirmed a seriousness of purpose about life. Quietly spoken, high-minded generations before ours had marked out these boundaries of an ordered, seemly life. It was all very private, very individual. Marriage seemed almost too worldly to impinge on this romanticism.

44

Yet one friend spoke to me of an older woman she had met in London: 'I can't bear the thought of that sort of rootless life–imagine, unmarried at forty–living in a bed sitting room ...' Then there was the afternoon I spent at an advertising agency, in half-hearted pursuit of a job. A depressing experience, and during the course of it I met Sarah. Only a year ago Sarah had been one of the beauties of Oxford, courted, successful, dazzling. Now she sat glumly before a typewriter, peevish and anonymous. There was also the story of someone's aunt. This aunt–I imagined a haggard woman with large spaniel's eyes–had refused too many proposals and missed her chance of marriage. At last, during the war, she had given herself to a man–once–in order not to die a virgin.

No wonder the end of our final year was celebrated with a rush of engagements and understandings. The brightly serious young women had intuitively understood a hidden purpose behind the aimless pleasure of the social round, had grasped the practicalities behind the privateness of love. Some of the most popular accepted proposals from unlikely men. I did not know the reasons and assumed that it had to do with a romantic passion that blew where it would, although it was a shock to observe one who was planning to marry a man with whom she was clearly not in love. I grasped only imperfectly the imperatives of adult life to which my contemporaries responded so gracefully. I was astonished, even contemptuous, when one of the stars of my year–she looked like a Rubens portrait, sumptuously pink and blonde–pronounced definitively against sex before marriage. I had scorned to save myself.

How many different ways are there of being naive? My morality might seem perverse and doomed, they idealistic in seeing in marriage a sexual transformation scene, a great consummation. They pledged their faith in marriage as the boundary to their world, to exclude disorder, to exclude the horror of a vacant future, the squalor of sex before

45

marriage, the mutilation that was virginity.

There *were* women in my college who were known to sleep with men. Two of these were pale and heavy lidded as if the weight of their sexual experience debilitated and wearied them. An air of the sluttish, a slip drooping below the hemline, smeared lipstick, armpit hair, marked them off as lost. One never opened the curtains of her room, and the dim room smelt always of stale cigarettes–a pudding basin stood on the table, a slag heap of ash and fag ends. My friend Jenny–Diana Dors–*looked* rosy and fresh as the Young Girls, but her room too was a slut's den of spilt nail varnish and used nylons, of bottles solid with bad milk unearthed from beneath piles of dirty clothes and old crusts of toast, with love letters carelessly left amongst essays and lecture notes, and lipsticks rolling out from under mould-caked cups and plates.

Her lover, Paul, seemed to me a far cry from the Boyish Undergraduate, counterpart of the Young Girl. He had nearly been expelled from school for wearing a green carnation in his lapel. He was reputed to have been an Existentialist in Paris and he was supposed to be brilliant academically. He used to appear silently in Jenny's room like a character out of a novel. Dressed in black polo neck and old jeans he muttered witticisms and discussed philosophy. He had what passed for long hair, a grown-out short back and sides, part of which hung in a lump over his long, melancholy face. He looked you deep in the eyes with his frightening pale ones, while maintaining a distance by his murmured utterances.

Forbidden, as my friend's lover, even if their affair was drawing to its end, he could fascinate me. I could even fall in love with his reputation as genius. But it was only the ghost of an affair. I could not *be* Jenny sexually any more than I had been able to *be* Barbara socially. These alternative identities remained theirs, not mine. 'Why can't we talk?' Paul would ask, bored by my wooden silences. It was all humiliating. I felt foolish, ultimately. There was neither pain nor blood from defloration, which was disappointing–I had expected a drama of bloodstained sheets. 'Who was there before me?' he murmured insistently– we knew the same people. My denial seemed absurd. How could I talk to him? Mulish, I remained silent also on the subject of my failure to experience sexual ecstasy.

But it was worth it for the triumph of losing my virginity. He called a taxi and gave me a ten shilling note with which to pay for it–a slightly shady transaction. The taxi drew up outside my house. I handed the driver the rust-coloured note: 'Keep the change,' I said, a gesture of magnificence and celebration–throwing money and caution to the winds.

There is romance in the way the glamorous disappear from their firmament, from your life. His First in Greats– Oxfordese for a first class degree in philosophy–achieved, Paul disappeared into national service, two years in the army seeming an inglorious and improbable fate. Later, even more improbably, he was said to have gone into business. A few more years and someone told me he was living in a crumbling house in South London and writing a book. Once, long after, I caught sight of him in an Algerian café in Paris. He hadn't changed. Now there was someone with identity!

I tried to make Paul, too, my identity. He, like me, I thought, craved excess and disdained the craven certainties of remaining within the middle class. His identity remained implacably clear, deadpan, while mine seemed amorphous and viscous. Yet his clarity was not the glassy certainty of the conformists, but the repose of the nihilist. And if, incidentally, individuals from the middle and upper classes are often said to have 'confidence'–usually held to be part of a strong sense of identity–this may be only because they have never been bumped against those invisible edges of social institutions and processes, have kept well inside the spaces–spacious enough after all–marked out for them in life, so that the identity has kept an apparent graceful fluidity expressed as social confidence and charm.

My contemporaries, the bright but serious young women, did have a strong sense of identity, which came from being at one with their social environment. They chose the path that had already been mapped out for them in life–and nothing gives a greater sense of freedom and expansion of self than plunging forward on well-oiled tracks. Their sense of identity had to do with identification with their class, and of identification with a special feminine role within that class. They were after all not to be just wives, but were to be diplomats' wives–or at least the wives of doctors, headmasters, vicars and stockbrokers.

So the boundary of class was to make our lives safe. Life was to be middle-class marriage–a spacious Park surrounded by a mossy wall. The ornamented gates, the avenues, the fountains and the vistas all demonstrated order. That at least is how I saw it. I realise in retrospect, though, that to many of my contemporaries it may have been a wild enough place, and indeed a great adventure into the unknown.

Was it enough? Was it real, even, the world of fresh-faced young men, eager with youthful passion, the world in which poetry mingled with fine sherry on the tongue? Madness and cruelty could hunt you down even here. I remember a dance at my college, and a woman don in tears because one of the fresh-faced young men had called her a dried up old virgin to her face. In the lavatories a bedraggled girl was being sick from drunkenness. I was too bright that evening, too high, squawking like a bird in my black taffeta dress and red shoes.

There was the violence of those who had been rejected in love. One crazed lover threw all his furniture out of his window. Another beat up his girl friend. A third killed himself.

48

Then there were the women dons and the women pursuing doctoral degrees, the higher learning. Some were too beautiful. Some dressed like men and smoked cheroots. They had no children, or their children were strange. Barbara's cruel gossip decreed this one lesbian, that one a fascist, a third had religious mania. The measure of things seemed to have come unsprung. The dreariness of unmarried women in bed sitting rooms haunted the Oxford suburbs. There was a life of popping gas fires, rickety chairs and single divans for the intellectual woman.

In horror, we fled the loneliness of those lives, flocking to the parties given by public school men in their old, lovely rooms in Meadow Buildings, Peckwater Quad, New Buildings, Oriel. The sound of Tommy Kinsman's band beat across the meadows near Magdalen. We waited for dawn to seep through the trees. Ball gowns were wet at the hems from dragging through the grass. This was Life–we had stayed up all night.

There was another world I dreamed of whose inhabitants lived by excess, lived for sensation, Paul's world, surely. He had bypassed this claustrophobic world with its obsessional class rituals. He wasn't frightened of facing the madness of excess.

But Oxford itself was mad, of course, riddled with the paranoia of young men in search of success and the hysteria of young women in search of love. We were all crazed with class–trying to merge its privilege and its rituals with its careful decency, that longing to be nice. The cultured cadence, the sharp sweetness of a turn of phrase, the liberal ideals–there was our pre-packaged identity, the identity of the civilised middle class.

Five

An identity that had its limitations–it fitted me in 1958 to become a publisher's secretary with a charming smile and a modicum of typing. My boss was like a nice father or a nice Oxford 'don'–dry distillation of class. But the atmosphere of Oxford withered in London: 'I'm so *bored.*' Boredom emptied London. Life became a gaping void. A nice girl in her high-heeled shoes and pale stockings–skirts were shorter that year–wandered through the vacant stucco vistas of West London, carrying a red book with its title in large letters across the cover: *Passion and Society.* 'I'll teach you more about that than any book,' shouted a passing lorry driver. Anything would be better than this. There must be some way to escape.

A new life–a new nightmare, not the white emptiness of London, but a Dickens world in which everyone lived by stereotype and became a caricature–a life in which I must become a caricature too.

*

The cottages of Fairlawns encircled a huge oval of grass, now parched and pale after the hot summer of 1959. Beyond them lay dark, glossy shrubs. But the attempt to create something halfway between model village cosiness and country house graciousness failed to conceal that Fairlawns was an institution.

When I met Matron her blank non-response to the smile and the bright manner I'd developed as a graduate-secretary hinted at new hidden edges of social norms. Massive, impersonal, colourless, yet formidable, she escorted me to the cottage where I was to work: 'There will be a lot of housework–you do realise that. Well I'm sure Mr

Partridge will have discussed this with you.' In fact the Superintendent had talked to me only of the emotional deprivation of the children in his care. His talk had been all of psychology and therapy.

We arrived at Rose Cottage. I was introduced to Auntie Maureen and Auntie Doris.

''Ee—but Elizabeth's such a mouthful, int' it,' cried Auntie Doris.

And so I was given another new identity: Auntie Liz. Auntie Maureen was as small and neat as a Dutch doll. Auntie Doris wiped large hands on her overall and pushed her hair back from her forehead.

'Yer done any o' this sort o' work before?' I shook my head and smiled my secretary's smile. Like Matron, she failed to respond.

'It's very 'ard work, yer know.'

Auntie Maureen showed me my room, a locked cubicle off the girls' dormitory. I sat on the bed. There was no room for my books, nor for my make-up. My clothes could hardly be crammed into the spindly cupboard. Someone thumped into the dormitory. Bedsprings twanged. There was muttering and whistling. Feeling shy, I came out of my room.

'Ooh—ooh,' the girl screamed with laughter, 'yer give me ever such a fright, creeping outa yer room like that. You our new Auntie?' She had the body almost of a young woman, but was dressed in frills, white cotton socks and sandals. She leaped against me so that I staggered, and kissed me wetly and noisily on the cheek.

'Cor, yer fragile, int yer Auntie—going ter show me yer room then? Oh go on—let me see yer make-up and that.' In a moment she was trying on my lipstick. Auntie Maureen appeared.

'You're not really supposed to be up here in the daytime, Abigail. You know that.'

'Auntie was lettin' me try 'er makeup.' Auntie Maureen

51

looked at me.

In the morning, I was sent to get the boys up. Greeted with a barrage of whistles, shouts and laughter my 'charming' smile somehow couldn't carry across the wall of noise. The older ones leapt from bed to bed, teased the little ones, told dirty jokes, got more and more excited. When Auntie Maureen came and told them it was disgraceful, I felt as much disgraced as they.

A noisy breakfast with fifteen children, most of whom had to be got off to school, left me exhausted by eight-thirty. Sent to clean upstairs, I sat down instead in my cubicle, read a little, went into a dream. The solitude was wonderful. When I started to sweep round the dormitories I felt bored. It was difficult to get all the dust from under the beds, and I didn't know what else I was supposed to do. There wasn't much to dust, and anyway I hadn't been given a duster.

'Here's your post.' Maureen stood in the doorway. 'You have got a lot of letters. You nearly finished up here?'

Clearly I hadn't, as I had to admit.

'Oh–' Auntie Maureen's smile didn't change, 'All right–you can finish after coffee. By the way–we don't call them dormitories, you know. I think it's more like home if we say bedrooms, don't you?' She looked round the room and went down the line of beds straightening the counterpanes and mats. 'Matron would have a fit if she saw the corners untucked like that,' she said, again in her colourlessly conversational tone of voice.

Auntie Doris stood at the kitchen table kneading pastry.

'You do have a lot of letters, don't yer. I never knew a person 'ave so many . . . Could you cut up the apples for this pie?'

When I'd cut them into thin, beautiful segments, she said: 'Well, there's no need to do them like that, yer know. We 'ave ter work quick in this job.'

''Ave ter be quick on the job, do yer Auntie,' shouted

52

Abigail from the doorway. They both roared with laughter.

I hated the vulgarity, the coarseness of the language, everything. All these bruised identities roughly jostling dissolved my identity under the onslaught of their collective one–exposure to their curiosity, quick affection, slow hostility. Abigail symbolised it all.

Cynical, wary, ready to resist being conned, they all saw my accent and manner as a kind of sell, an elaborate insult almost, a way of poking fun at them, as well as a claim to some superiority to which I clearly had no right. At best, I was an eccentric, at worst a prig, this 'I' that they saw being a complete class stereotype. And as the intimacy of this strange new life began to tear off the Oxford veneer, which seemed to them so intolerably affected, I became conscious of my new identity, Auntie Liz, as a slovenly, untidy, lacklustre young woman, who was depressed, and couldn't keep order, who was as nervous of Auntie Doris and Auntie Maureen as she was of the children, and who therefore tried to placate and, like Abigail–the other 'new girl'–ingratiate.

*

George, the only Fairlawns grammar school boy, was in Rose Cottage, and Mr Partridge had suggested I encourage him in his work. He hoped George might go to university.

'University? 'E's bloomin' nuts, not bleeding likely, nothing but bleedin' exams ... I'm gonna leave 'ere, goin' in wiv me dad next year, bookie 'e is. Money in that.'

I tried to talk to him about the 'fun' and 'marvellous times' you could have at university.

'Oh yeah? You was at Oxford an' all wasn't yer? Mr Partridge come down an' told Maureen, full of it 'e was. Can't talk about nothing but education, full of big ideas 'e is. Not for me, though–don't get paid, do yer, not like a job.'

I told him it would be worth it in the end.

'Well–don't seem to 'ave got you so far–what you doin' down 'ere then?'

George was the focus of unspoken tension. Auntie Maureen said of him:

'You should have seen my eldest boy, Roger. Now Roger really *was* a nice boy, oh he was so polite and helpful, I had more time for him than I have for George–ever so much more. George isn't–I don't think he's got it in him . . . He's ever so lazy. It's not a bit the same without Roger. You'd have liked him . . . This was a nice cottage when Roger was here–the best cottage in Fairlawns, Mr Partridge thought. Doris is ever such a good worker, and the assistant we had before you, Giulietta, she was a wonderful girl. Italian she was.'

A week or so later George showed me his new lighter: 'Friend give it me–from Ireland.' He winked. Afterwards Auntie Maureen said:

'I know where he got that from. Ridiculous giving a boy his age an expensive lighter.'

After lunch George said:

'I'm goin' over ter Lavender ter see Rusty. Okay?'

'Yes, you may leave the table George.'

'That boy near lives in Lavender.' Doris laughed. Maureen frowned.

'Well, if he wants to live there he can, so far as I'm concerned. There's many over there would change places I'm sure.'

There was a chorus of agreement from the children. One boy said: ''S'bloomin' 'orrible over there–my sister was with *'er* an' all.'

'If you mean Miss Armstrong, say so, don't say 'her', it's rude.' And Auntie Maureen turned to me with a rare and unexpected explanation. 'Miss Armstrong's a very old-fashioned housemother, she's ever so strict with the children, much too strict, really, they're a downtrodden lot over there, aren't they Doris?'

'Ee, they are downtrodden, I should say so, yer don't want ter be over there.'

Was Rusty one of the boys at Lavender Cottage?

'No–that Miss O'Riordan he means, the deputy.'

*

Abigail and I–victim and tormenter, flaming egos, locked
in battle, 'caring person' and 'deprived child', street child
and middle-class miss–I was undone by my longing to be
nice. She sneered at me. I feared and hated her.

No one could control Abigail. Her mood swung dangerously between hilarity and violence, with never a point of
rest in between–everything carried to instant excess in a
kind of malign, desperate hysteria. She grasped the essentials of every situation and quickly caricatured it. The
exaggeration of her own moods and her electric sensing of
the moods of others produced a lightning field of hysteria. I
was an easy target:

'Hey you–Liz–bottle legs, look at 'er 'air, like a bird's
nest, ooh–you got nits or something?–ooh, yer going ter
cry? Go on–'

She egged the 'little ones' on–I was desperate for them to like
me–so that they 'played up'. There were scenes. I hit them.

'Oh I say, yer shouldn't have done that, yer know' cried
Doris. 'Yer want to go to a cottage like Lavender if yer like
hitting children. It isn't just a matter of tucking them up in
bed and reading ter them yer know–more like 'ard work.'

The next day, a Sunday, the children were dressed in
their best to go to church.

'Doesn't ours look a nice family,' said Auntie Maureen,
'It really does, it looks ever such a nice family. I think it's a
nice idea, don't you, that we should all dress up and look
our best to go to church on Sunday?'

'I don't believe in God,' I said, 'I can't see the point–what
does it mean to the children? It seems so conformist to
dress them all up like this–why can't they be out playing or
reading or something?'

Maureen stared at me expressionlessly: 'These children
don't read.'

55

In the evening we drank our coffee after the children had gone to bed. Doris said: 'I'm about at the end of my tether, Maureen–that Abigail's getting beyond anything yer know. This place is bedlam with 'er around. And when's Mr Partridge goin' ter get 'er another school–there don't seem no sign of *that,* for all 'is talk ...'

'Yes. It can't go on. The cottage is just going down and down. And when I think what a nice cottage this used to be. Mr Partridge'll have to move her.'

'Shame in a way,' said Doris with a sudden grin. 'But she is a funny girl, oh she is a moody girl. But d'you know I still can't 'elp liking 'er in a way? She 'as got a sense of humour at least, more than what some people 'ave.'

In the morning Auntie Maureen went to the office to see Mr Partridge about having Abigail moved to another cottage. In the afternoon I spent my free time sitting in my messy cubicle. A tap on the door–it was Matron.

'I should like to have a word with you Miss Wilson. May I come in?'

I swept dirty underwear off a chair.

'I've come to tell you we've decided to move you to another cottage. We feel the time has come to show you a different way of doing things, Miss Wilson. We're going to put you in Lavender Cottage, with Miss Armstrong. She'll show you another way. You'll find it different there.' After a silence she said: 'I don't know if you have anything to say, Miss Wilson? ... No? ... Well–tomorrow morning you'll start at Lavender. Is that all right then, Miss Wilson? Very well then–if I were you I should tidy up this room. It's in an awful mess, isn't it?'

*

'Miss Wilson, will you sit at the head of that table there, please? Right.' Miss Armstrong's small hands twitched down at her sides. She waited. There was a moment's dead silence.

'Somebody,' said Miss Armstrong in a ringing Yorkshire

56

voice, 'has done something *disgusting* in the lavatory. Something has been *smeared* all over the walls. Now you are all going to stand there until the boy or girl who did this disgusting thing comes out here and owns up to me. *I* don't care if you're late for school, Monica, so it's no good putting that face on. It's entirely up to the person concerned whether they want to keep us waiting here all morning or not.'

Silence. Then a small boy crept out from behind his table and towards Miss Armstrong.

'Leroy. I *thought* so. Very well. Come outside with me. And after breakfast you can clean it up and you can go to school late, and you can explain to your teacher exactly *why* you are late, and you had better tell her the truth, because I shall make it my business to ask her just what you did tell her. Rusty—will you say grace, please.'

Rusty had her back to Miss Armstrong and gave the children a terrific wink. She gabbled grace. Chairs scraped back, but then instead of the barrage of voices I'd expected, silence fell. Rusty and I served porridge. From the bathroom we could still hear Miss Armstrong's voice.

'Right—bend over the bath, Leroy.'

The child whimpered.

'*Now* then.'

A yell followed each blow and at the end there was a volley of sobs.

After breakfast Miss Armstrong gave me detailed orders: 'Now Miss Wilson, I want you to go upstairs and sweep out the dormitories thoroughly, and dust them, and I want the floors up there polished if you please. Then you can sweep and wash down the stairs and scrub the bathroom floor. These things have to be done every day, otherwise the place gets filthy with fifteen pairs of dirty shoes in and out all the time, don't you agree? I shall expect all that done before we stop at half-past ten for coffee.'

At least I now knew what was expected of me, and to

57

work really hard was more enjoyable than when I'd trailed round the dormitories in Rose at a snail's pace. We sat round the kitchen table for a proper coffee break at precisely half past ten. Miss Armstrong initiated a discussion of the news, reading out headlines from the *News Chronicle*.

'Orrh, 'tis terrible, Miss Armstrong,' said Rusty, and picked her teeth as she stared ahead, blank-eyed. I sipped the real coffee–there were chocolate biscuits too.

'I like a good cup of coffee, don't you, Miss Wilson? I always have preferred it to tea, have I.'

'Orrh but it's a wonderful thing, a cup of strong tea,' said Rusty, 'makes you feel reely grand.'

After lunch she sat with me, while I darned the socks Miss Armstrong had given me.

'Here–have a fag now she's gone. She hates it. Mind you, she can't reely stop us in here now, but if she catches you at it in the kitchen–why she'll kill yer ... Still–she has a terrible reputation, yer know, has auld Sarah, but she's not a bad auld thing reely to tell ye the truth. O' course Mr Partridge, he hates the sight o' her now, so I don't suppose ye'd a good word said about her over there.' And she jerked her mahogany-coloured curls in the direction of Rose. 'That Maureen Owen's one of his little pets. Makes yer sick. They say she's ever so two-faced an' all, goin' up there and complaining to him about you behind yer back. Wit' that divil of a girl in there an' all. Was a shame reely.' She puffed blankly at her fag, but just as I prepared to unburden myself she sprang to her feet, cried, 'Orrh well, ye'll die if ye worry, ye'll die if ye don't so why worry at all!' and, cup in hand, she tilted away on her long straight legs and stiletto heels.

My new life had a fixed routine. I rose at dawn, put the big kettle on to boil and lit the gas beneath the double saucepan of porridge. Then I battled with the boiler in its gritty antechamber off the kitchen, banging the poker round in its slot and rattling it up and down to loosen the cinders. These I carried before me in a still smouldering heap along the passage and out of the back door, seized the lid from the dustbin and turning my face away quickly reversed them into the bin and banged the lid back, but never in time to prevent the ash blinding up in my face and over my hair. Then I hurried indoors again to my worst task–to light the dayroom fire. Miss Armstrong had shown me how to do it, and made it seem easy with a triumphant flourish of the wrist, but often I had to try several times before I managed to get it going. Miss Armstrong wouldn't allow the use of anything so extravagant and unnecessary as firelighters, which had been freely used in Rose.

Then I heard Miss Armstrong's voice upstairs: '*Now* then, children–*if* you please–*up*!'

The bedwetters came scampering down to take cold baths. I was cutting slice after slice of bread. Brian, back from his paper round, slung his bike against the wall by the back door and came into the kitchen to share our early tea. That was one of the many small customs and routines whereby Miss Armstrong had stamped the life of Lavender Cottage with a pattern of her own, a routine quite lacking in Rose, where it had been spontaneity that was prized. Now she stalked into the kitchen and poured the tea I'd made. She and I remained in the kitchen, apart from the quiet, desperate rushing up and down stairs.

'And what's the news today, Brian? Have they blown up the world yet?'

'Oh no, Miss.' Brian, red-nosed, whey-faced, held his hands to warm round his cup and grinned. He was fond of Miss Armstrong.

Now I had to cook breakfast. The bacon and slices of bread must be quickly fried in smoking hot fat. But cooking was one thing I was good at.

The two little girls of the cottage came in to have their hair plaited. Miss Armstrong tied the huge, crisp bows

59

with her usual flourish, pulling the ribbon so that the knots zipped tight with a little whine.

On the days when Rusty was in charge there was a different, gay, reckless atmosphere:

'And the top o' the morning to ye!'

There was giggling and laughing upstairs, and pushing as well as scurrying in the passage.

'Get a move on, you children! Look sharp now—not so much noise, thank ye, unless you want to be waking Miss Armstrong—I'm thinking 'twas a full moon last night, Gracie Hobson, by the way ye're carryin' on—did ye' ever see the like of it! The girl's mad! That's a lovely plate of fried bread ye've done there Liz—I can't stand the sight o' the stuff meself, and nor can the kids, only for her we'd never have it—still ye'll die if ye worry, and ye'll die if ye don't, so why worry at all!'

And the children would say: 'Rusty's in charge today, int she, Miss. Ooh smashing. Smashing int it, Miss, when Rusty's in charge. Eh Miss!'

Yet we all knew that the licentious days when Miss Armstrong was 'off' formed a recognised part of the pattern, her pattern, and that its natural and inevitable counterpart was the sterner routine of the days when she was 'on'. So there it was, a strange fellowship, with self-protection hardening caricature into carapace. Rusty sent herself up as a warm-hearted stage Irish—Irish as no person really ever was. Miss Armstrong was held in the vice of her steel corset of self-control, a stereotype, textbook dragon.

*

Miss Armstrong received Matron behind closed doors one December afternoon. In the evening we sat round the kitchen table for the quiet coffee hour I enjoyed. Miss Armstrong cut fruit cake.

'I expect you'll be wondering why Matron called in here—it seems we're to have this girl Abigail over from Rose. That Auntie Doris or whatever she calls herself doesn't seem able to cope with her now that Miss Owen's left . . . so they've decided *we* can look after her! I told Matron what I thought of it, oh yes. They all try out their new-fangled ways with these 'emotionally disturbed' children! And then, when they've had enough–who gets them? Now if I'd had this girl from the start, mind you, I don't say it'd have been easy, but if I'd had her from the start, there'd not have been all this trouble.

'And another thing, Matron, I said. It's not fair on my assistant. Miss Wilson had all that trouble with the girl over in Rose Cottage, and now she's just trying to live it down over here when the girl's sent after her. Well it's true, Elizabeth. I consider it most unfair on you. You may or may not have turned out a good assistant, it's too early to say, but it's not giving you a chance sending this girl over here after you. She'll think you're easy game, she'll think she got you out of one cottage, she can get you out of another. Well we're not having any of that here. She may have upset that silly Miss Owen in Rose, but I'm not having it in *my* cottage. So *now* then. Mr Partridge still thinks it can all be done with love of course. Love! I don't know what this place is coming to, no really I *don't*. Soppy, I call it. They need firmness and discipline, these girls. They respect you for that. Not all this sloppy sentimentality. Just you remember that, Miss Wilson. Don't sink to their level–rise above it, live it down, that's my advice to you.'

Lying in the darkness at night–my interview with Mr Partridge: 'When I came here I found segregation by age and sex, no family homes, rigid discipline, uniforms, the cane . . . I had those children up here and I spoke to them, all of them. This is your home, I said . . . the bad old days are over.'

I believed in all those things myself, that is I abhorred 'discipline' and believed in understanding. But what have ideals and beliefs to do with the self, a huddled shapeless thing beneath the heavy bedclothes? Identity broke down to a jelly, an infant core.

On the evening of Abigail's arrival Miss Armstrong presided, benevolent but alert, over Welsh Rarebit and Ovaltine. We all knew why the supper was an especially nice one.

'Thought you said the new girl was coming, Miss.'

'Well, that's what I was told, but she hasn't turned up, has she, Monica? Perhaps she didn't like the sound of we.'

They tittered. Gracie squirmed and made a face.

'What'll you do, Miss, if she don't come?'

'Do? *Do*? I shan't do anything, Gracie. What do you want me to do? Go over and fetch her?'

'Ooh, no Miss, no, go and fetch her, ooh no.' Gracie broke into her mad, spiralling laughter. Rusty caught my eye. Soon we should all be in fits of nervous giggles.

'*Now* then!' Miss Armstrong brought us to order. 'That's enough Gracie. Don't you go having one of your turns. You've no need. You can be quite sensible when you try.'

'Yes Miss.' She clapped her hand over her mouth, her eyes round and big above it.

There was a bang on the door.

'Well! 'Ere I am, folks. Evening all!'

Abigail had a big grin for us all; the old trooper, the clown. Big feet stuck out, she clumped round the table.

At first she kept quiet, and seemed to settle into her new school and into Lavender. And Rusty said: 'The girl's got a sense o' humour now, ye have to admit, poor thing, ugly lump of a thing that she is.'

But soon, on Miss Armstrong's days off, Abigail began to circle round me again, muttering to the rest: 'Don't take any notice of 'er, she's only a skivvy, she's a nutter she is ...' And the children sensed my change of mood, my irritability and depression, my fear of becoming a scapegoat once more:

62

'Er, Miss, yer always moaning these days, Miss.'

'Yeah, 'orrible when she moans, int it.'

Everyone was tense. Abigail affected us like an un-exploded bomb. And she soon ceased to be on her best behaviour. She capered round the cottage in the evenings and even Miss Armstrong's bugle shouts couldn't keep her quiet. Each evening, even in Miss Armstrong's presence, the air of licence heightened into anarchy and insolence as Abigail swung from room to room at will, laughing and joking at first but gradually working herself up into a state of high tension that could only resolve itself in shouting and screaming. She no longer trod carefully in Lavender, but rounded on us all. She could not be controlled. She was once more excluded from school. So then she crouched at home all day by the fire, refused to eat her meals and laughed in Miss Armstrong's face, dismissive of the strength of will by which Miss Armstrong ruled the other children.

'She'll get rid of her now,' muttered Rusty, 'ye'll see–now the girl's defied her, that's the finish. Only for that ye'd have had her here indefinite.'

Uproar–a sense of impending violence–yes, she had to go. That boisterousness, that 'sense of humour'–why did they always change to desperate, mad confrontation? No one at Fairlawns had time to understand her. Abigail, the joker of the pack, the fool always about to step off a precipice, held up a distorting glass to me–I saw identity dissolve into fear, violence, shame.

On her last evening she was violently sick, but she came downstairs in her pyjamas and pranced round the dayroom in an attempt to reassert her ascendancy over the children, who had grown tired of her by now. She was the old entertainer who could no longer get a laugh from the audience. She grovelled, sweated her guts out, talked herself hoarse to raise a laugh, but they wouldn't respond. For ultimately they distrusted her violence. She went too

63

far. Little old men and women before their time, they preferred a quiet life, preferred, for that matter, the strict routine of Miss Armstrong to the licence of Rusty: 'at least you know where you are with old Sarah,' the older children said.

So Abigail came into the kitchen. It was Shrove Tuesday. We were eating pancakes as Miss Armstrong made them, one by one. Rusty was ironing, and Abigail cried:

'Eh, look at old Rusty there, dashin' away with the smoothing iron–' And suddenly she had us all laughing with her again and there was a moment's warmth and sympathy for Abigail now that we knew she was leaving.

She left, but nothing changed. Rusty said: 'She was a laugh that girl, ye have to admit. 'Twas too bad she had such a down on ye, only for that ... Though to be quite honest, auld Sarah thought you were hopeless wit' the girl. I'm sorry, but she did. Yer let them get under yer skin too much, if ye'll excuse me for sayin' so. Ye shouldn't take a blind bit o' notice of all their cheek. And ye should never let them see ye're frightened of them, never. Ye've *had* it then, oh no, I'm sorry but that's absolutely fatal ... Well, yer don't seem any too pleased the girl's gone, Liz. Ye're ever so moody, aren't ye, I reely can't understand you at times.'

Miss Armstrong's attitude towards me had hardened when Abigail arrived in Lavender, but she did not become pleasanter once Abigail had left. On the contrary, she was always finding fault.

'Someone has been smoking in here. Now I've told you before, Elizabeth, I will not have smoking in the kitchen. It's against the regulations and it's very unhygienic and you are not to do it. Now do you *hear* me?'

'There's no need to shout, I'm not deaf.'

'And there's no need to be rude. I asked a question and I want an answer.'

'Well don't speak to me as if I were one of the children then.'

'Ah! Well then don't you behave as if you were one of the children, Miss Wilson, that's what I have to say to you. So now then! And as for that, the children have no respect for you in any case, none whatever. The way you follow that Rusty like a silly sheep–an educated girl like yourself, or supposed to be, to allow a woman like Rusty to get such an ascendancy over you the way she has. She twists you right round her little finger with all that Irish flattery–for that's all it is, you know. She doesn't like you–oh, you should hear the things she has to say about you behind your back, young lady. She hasn't a good word to say for you then. I should *never* have thought it of a girl from a decent background, as I supposed you to be. No pride–no standards. Oh–you blamed Abigail for all your troubles, but I can tell you, you've been more trouble to me than ever Abigail was–yes–you give yourself such airs, but–'

'I've never given myself airs. It's been all the rest of you who've assumed–'

'You and your soppy talk–Just like Mr Partridge and his little dears. All this talk about love! As though it were some kind of patent medicine. Well, I don't see much love in the way you treat these children. No I don't.'

And now we were shouting at each other, both hysterical. It was like an adolescent quarrel with my mother.

In the evening Rusty cheered me up with a fag.

'Come on now, it's not as bad as all that. The auld cow has to take it out on someone–*she* feels she's failed wit' Abigail too, ye know.'

*

Where would Abigail be now? At Fairlawns my alter ego (neither of us could cope with the place) never seen from that day to this–at some level her violence was exciting. The brink, the precipice, the edge–what happened to identity then? Which was worse (or better?), to smash it into smithereens of violence or dissolve it in a grin of fear?

I left. I had dinner with an old flame in Soho. An Oxford aesthete who'd affected a silver-headed cane and brocade waistcoats, his accent and conversation jarred. (All the 'effing and blinding' had knocked the edges off my brittle glass voice.) Still in love with Oxford, he was forging ahead in business.

'You've changed,' he kept saying, with a puzzled disapproving frown. He wanted Glynis Johns the undergraduette back sitting opposite him. But Fairlawns had splintered her to bits.

'Ah, the real world, the real world,' he sighed, nostalgic for afternoons in punts. He willed his definition of my identity onto me but he couldn't compete with the collective will of Fairlawns, which had revealed a different self, I wasn't sure what. But I felt he was clinging to an outworn self, while I was in a hurry to get on to something new. To have actually survived Fairlawns, however ingloriously, somehow gave me a firmer identity. Against his mannerisms I measured the distance I felt I'd travelled.

Six

A year later, and it was summer again in Oxford, 1961. On a weekend visit I walked alone in the Parks before breakfast. The sky was already a hot blue. I was in love.

Later we plunged between bramble hedges and past dusty nettles to reach an overgrown garden belonging to some friends. North Oxford–doors stood open to untidy rooms. The house was dark, cool, hollow. The young woman lay on a broken-down chaise longue and clasped her stomach in anguish: 'It's kicking.' Her small child staggered to and fro with his potty, reluctant either to use it or let it go. He climbed on to the low garden table and shat near a plate of roast beef. We talked to the husband as we ate lunch, but motherhood seemed to have claimed the wife.

Here was heterosexual marriage. It seemed like an unexpected disaster, painful and chaotic, far removed from the ideal lesbian relationship that *we* had just established. None of us had yet reached twenty-five, yet although I felt we were all still on the threshold of life, already we were hurtling down paths we hardly knew we had chosen.

*

The adults had often asked Chatterbox and the selves that followed her: What do you want to be when you grow up? That they asked what she wanted to *be* rather than *do* hints at the extent to which identity is defined by work. You can only 'be' what you do–you cannot have an identity just by being. Alienation and 'loss of identity' come in the modern world from loss of meaningful work–or so they say.

Chatterbox had wanted to be in the circus. If she could

67

be a circus star she would recapture that wonderful afternoon at the circus when she had been carried away by the smell of sawdust, by the sight of snorting ponies, by the yellow lights and hoarse music. Chatterbox had planned to spend her life wonderful in a pink tutu, poised on one toe on the back of one of those ponies, carried away on the swooping, triumphant dance of pleasure, a fixed smile painted on her face. She had even experienced that exhilaration once when, in her white organdie bridesmaid's dress, its frills cascading to the ground, she'd won a prize for dancing the polka.

But Chatterbox had long since disappeared. A prim little girl in check gingham, sandals and blazer, her hair in plaits, played chess with her grandfather. At other times she sat at his formidably erect typewriter with its skeletal sunburst of keys. She tried to write an adventure story in the manner of Enid Blyton. She decorated the chapter headings with capitals 'illuminated' in red, green and turquoise-blue ink. But the plot posed problems. Later imitations, of E. Nesbit, of Baroness Orczy, of Jane Austen even, met with the same problem of how to make things happen.

In summer, she and her grandfather collected butterflies. Her grandfather chloroformed them in the stifling death chamber of a jam jar. They were pinned with their illuminated wings outstretched in a cork-lined box.

The little girl vanished, to be replaced by the ghost in Harrods, by Glynis Johns, by Auntie Liz in messy overalls and untidy 'beehive' hairstyle. Was it a personality, these layers of sediment cooling and hardening?

The adult self was certainly layered, or several-faced, different identities in one. I was for instance, a solitary self, full of a sense of identity. Energetic yet aimless I roamed London, and, alone in the crowd, in the mass of the great city, I was free. I was what Baudelaire called a *flâneur*, a word impossible to translate. I was visible to all, yet veiled in my anonymity. Passing swiftly by, I could inflame the desires of men without being touched by them. I could maintain an 'aristocratic' stance to life, preserving, no matter that I was alone, unaccompanied, unrecognised, a correctness of appearance, a perfect politeness to the humblest.

I was a creature whom only the perpetual excitement, the stimulation, the over-irritation of the metropolis can create, the Dandy, blasé yet longing to astonish. I fixed myself, like a chloroformed butterfly, on the shimmering surface of city life, extravagant, eccentric, distancing myself in order to 'be different'.

I'm just an aesthete, I said in rebellion against sensible, plodding daily identities I was being constrained to acquire. Yet secretly this identity dissatisfied me. It was the identity of a poseuse. A dandy is essentially someone who just *is* rather than someone who *does.* For an identity to have depth, it needs an active, moral dimension. The performer-identities Chatterbox had loved might have straddled the divide between acting and being, but undiluted dandyism was brittle, amoral, a performance without an audience other than the narcissistic audience of the self.

On a sunny day in 1961, when I was twenty-four and happy from falling in love, I bought a typewriter, carried it home and sat down to write. I am not clear what prompted this impulse. I think it may have been no more than a few words of praise for my prose style from a tutor. But, being as I was in search of an Identity, I was not content simply to sit down and explore the possibilities of writing, but had to turn this activity into a full-blown Identity.

A spontaneous urge to write is one thing. The wish to be a Writer is another. There was an innocent excitement in the expedition to buy the typewriter. To sit down and roll the first empty page into the machine felt positively virtuous. But the innocence, the purposefulness were soon sullied by a kind of shame. To 'write' (active) was to affirm a self more 'real' than the work identities so far offered. It appeared as an obscure and dedicated vocation that raised uncomfortable questions. What did you want to write about? Had you anything to say? What was the point of it? It evoked self doubt rather than identity. At the same time it was arrogant, since you were laying claim to talent, you were presuming to be a special sort of person, a capital-A Artist.

The wish to be a Writer (passive) was—even more meretricious—to claim a role, to admit that you wanted to show off to an audience, to be an adult Chatterbox in icing-sugar tulle. It simply betrayed a thirst for applause.

Also, the banality of it was revealed as the precious secret, leaked to a few chosen friends, turned out to be no heroic and unusual choice, but the secret self of a dozen friends and acquaintances. Everyone to whom you spoke seemed to be grabbing this particular identity, which made it seem more like the revelation of a hidden, minor but embarrassing deformity or disfigurement than the unveiling of a more real self, a more beautiful self. It was a skeleton in the cupboard, but one to which you had to confess. Impossible to keep it a secret—every so often it had to be ritually revealed to some chosen confidant, which proved that you were not endeavouring to follow a vocation but were hungry for an audience to give your chosen role the true ring of identity.

It almost felt as if this particular piece of self revelation were the intellectual equivalent of making a pass at someone: 'Actually–' (gulp) 'I'm—writing a novel.' It was like pouncing on the object of your desire after one of those heavy, alert silences that accompanied youthful seductions. It forced intimacy onto a new plane. And indeed rejection of the proffered secret—refusal, that is, in the shape of indifference or reluctance to be impressed, or to read your work—could be as much of a blow to friendship as a rejected kiss to romance.

There was also the hope that in claiming the identity Writer I would forge an entry to the sophisticated bohemia that I imagined existed just behind the surface of the London over which I glided without leaving any mark behind me. I sat hopefully in Soho coffee bars–but no one ever discovered me. I hunted for bargains amongst the bric-à-brac of the Portobello Road market on Saturday afternoons–but no one recognised me as a fellow bohemian. In those days an unrenovated Henekey's pub near the top of the market was haunted by arty-looking men and women. I used to sit in the back room which was furnished with old round tables and bentwood chairs before such furniture became fashionable. Stallholders and art students sat drinking hot toddies, and the atmosphere was closer to that of a French café than an English pub. But I was part of no group, no coterie of Artists.

In the autumn of 1961 my lover and I moved into a flat in North Gower Street. She had a new job, I was about to train as a social worker.

The back window looked out over Tolmer Square, now demolished, a circle of huge, decaying Regency houses surrounding a fleapit cinema. Tramps pissed against its walls. Asian families lived in the narrow houses above the Halal butchers and Indian restaurants in the surrounding streets. Who came and went in the hotels no one knew. At weekends the place was dusty and quiet. It was almost Bloomsbury, and a suitably seedy spot for a bohemian, a dandy, a writer to live.

The word bohemian, which has long since passed from my vocabulary, seemed right at the time, and redolent of the only atmosphere that might pass in those days for an alternative lifestyle. The bohemian lifestyle of the late fifties and early sixties could be lived out most fully–I imagined–only in the cafés of Paris or Greenwich Village. In it I should have played the part not so much of Writer, of Artist in my own right, but rather of Great Artist's

71

Mistress. Simone de Beauvoir, of course, was both. 'Mistress'—which now seems an Edwardian word, and stuffy in its implications of the double standard—then seemed suffused with the magic of a rebellious destiny. It was perhaps how our friend Maurice would have more easily understood me.

His Roman, noble head and heavy torso were set on thin legs, and this violently present, top-heavy body well expressed his intensity and emotionalism. He gave me *The White Goddess* by Robert Graves, which fitted his own vision of Woman as goddess and earth-mother. As Artist's-mistress, I should have fitted this vision, as Writer I was too intellectual. He was an embryo art critic and poet, but there was never any sense of a shared literary destiny. Maleness and Femaleness got in the way of that. Maurice did not know whether to be in love with me or with my girl friend, or with other tense and earnest young women who came and went in his life. I remained obstinately not a goddess, resolutely continued to wear black leather and tight black trousers and dandified frills. But he raised an awkward question in my mind. What gender was the Writer?

Maurice introduced us to Percy, who revealed another side to the writer's life. We visited his seedy corner of West London, waited ages for him to answer the door. At last it opened, and a sallow man with huge, mournful eyes peered out. It was mid afternoon, but he wore an old velvet dressing gown:

'Hello! Kept you waiting did I? To be perfectly frank, I was on the bog!' His laughter exploded in a fart of derision.

We went upstairs and sat in what seemed like the dressing room of a faded actress, with tarnished brocade and souvenirs, and cards around the walls—'my tat' as he called it. Percy, I was to learn, often hovered behind the net curtains, a carp floating in the dusty light, his element of bored anxiety.

In the life of those years, in my slightly arid and depressed twenties, he was a romantic figure. Twice my age, divorced, and a writer, he wanted to marry me–he said. His bohemian existence fascinated me. His moods of anxiety, of manic perkiness, of cynicism, the alternate states of comparative wealth and of living from hand to mouth, the moments when he had an idea and the times when he was becalmed, artistically, all had the charm of the exotic to me with my too rooted life.

He took me to dockland pubs where men danced with other men–a strange and menacing scene. He took me to East End Chinese restaurants which were like cheap caffs, apart from the food; he took me to drag shows and boxing matches. This was a male sweat underworld of risk and violence, though sexually ambiguous too. But then Percy liked anything that was a bit off, a bit camp. Maybe that's why he liked me.

He admired 'little masterpieces', and introduced me to the works of writers such as Jean Rhys–then almost unknown–and J. R. Ackerley. Perhaps he hoped to write what he called a 'little gem' himself one day. His approach to writing was wholly professional, though, and he would have no truck with grand ideas about identity and aspiration: 'Writing's a craft–d'you know that–a craft. The challenge is to take an idea, any idea, and work it up into something. Take this film script I'm working on at the moment–the story's a load of *shit,* it really is–no, I mean that–but a really professional writer can make something of anything–anything–doesn't matter what it is. Take a thriller, for instance–a really good writer can do *wonders* with a perfectly ordinary little plot for a thriller . . . So how about *that* then!'

His mother had been a milliner in the East End, and when he talked about writing he reminded me of his descriptions of her transforming a drab straw hat by mounting on it an artificial flower, to create a little miracle

of chic for its delighted wearer. He despised my amateurish-
ness, and for him as for Maurice it was as a woman that I
was somehow, obscurely, unfitted for writing. It was not
that he had anything in theory against women writers, but
I did not *interest* him as a Writer. Rather I menaced him as
Woman, an identity that, so far as he was concerned, quite
overshadowed any other. I was simply one of a series of
women who were to save him from his lonely bohemianism.
Each was introduced into his life with the threatening:
'She's got that neurotic *warmth,* you know.' In each case
the warmth evaporated, and an inner coldness would
inevitably be revealed. And in my case, my claim to
'Writer' somehow became proof of my coldness–or so I felt.

The community of bohemians that would confirm my
identity–perhaps they were to be found in the lesbian clubs
to which my lover and I went in search, also, of social
confirmation of our relationship. We were never entirely at
ease in this basement world. The scene was not, as I'd
imagined, one of red plush sofas and Toulouse-Lautrec
tarts hunched over absinthe, but of bouffant hairstyles and
sharply creased trousers. I have memories of pale apricot
lipstick and thick black eyeliner, of carefully-not-quite-
butch black leather jackets and open-necked shirts, a world
of casual appearances and tight-lipped gentility. There was
a rough edge to it all–heavy, butch women who sometimes
got into fights. You sensed an underworld out of sight–
drugs, petty crime, prostitution maybe–but it was never
here. On the contrary the clubs were remarkable for their
respectability. At one or two parties I glimpsed the edge of
a territory where a world of privilege and a demi-monde
mingled, a rich woman's Mayfair pad, full of rococo
mirrors–huge rooms, bottles of whisky on a grand piano–
one of the guests was a professional Soho stripper and
began to get into her act. Or another party, this time in
Chelsea, where I found a deserted kitchen–a brace of
pheasants, out of season peaches, five-pound notes litter-

ing the table, while upstairs women, hoydenish and uncouth, made merry, oblivious of the Chippendale and the works of art.

There were little coteries of lesbians who aspired to write or paint. Some of them lived in interesting, potentially bohemian parts of London–Soho, Clerkenwell. We struck up a friendship with Jos and Lucy. They, like us, or like me at least, aspired to a lifestyle worthy of Jos's status as would-be Writer, to a life that was creative and sincere. Their flat, in a rickety Georgian house near St Bartholemew's Hospital, was, like our own, casually tasteful, with a lot of white paint and one standard Thames green wall in the living room, unmistakably early sixties. They played Mozart and Johnny Mathis records when we went round. They attended psychology courses some evenings, and Lucy translated poetry from French. Jos was working on a novel. Paradoxically, both worked during the week for one of the most conformist and traditional of the women's magazines.

Soon I had made my gushing, guilty secret confession to Jos, and there followed the exchange of strained, wan narratives–faded *because* they were about lesbians, some-how. There was an embarrassment about it all, partly because the hoped-for communion of Artists was muddled by uncertainties about gender. Who was masculine and who feminine in this relationship? Jos was, as it happened, more clearly defined as the dominant partner in her relationship with Lucy who was Artist's Mistress par excellence; my status fluctuated and was unclear.

Our relationship with Jos and Lucy was symbolically tremendously important to me for several years, because I sought in it an affirmation of more than one identity. They accepted me, didn't they, as a lesbian, as a Writer? But, although well meaning, the friendship was based on a kind of falsity, because we felt ambivalent towards their playing out of masculine and feminine roles–not unusual among

75

lesbians, although by no means universal, but for us a source of discomfort. And then, through knowing them I came to understand that writing, homosexuality and the *vie de Bohème* did not inevitably lead, as I'd always imagined, to socialism. Jos and Lucy 'adopted' an old man who was a neighbour of theirs and whose mother had died. He was lost and confused, since he'd lived with her all his life. He was removed and taken to an old workhouse now turned, rather ineffectively it seemed, into an old people's home, but was rescued by Jos and Lucy, who gave him Sunday dinners and generally kept an eye on him. My lover and I, it must be said, did not perform kindly acts like this. However, we were left-wing, weren't we, and they were not. So other identities could not be confirmed. But it was particularly the roles of male and female that caused an inescapable unease.

There was a similar problem with Danny, who had actually had a number of popular historical novels published. As with most of our friends, my statement that I was or wanted to be a Writer triggered off in her a response as if to the challenge of some obscure gender boundary. So far as Danny was concerned I was defined as Femininity. She liked to talk about the 'mysteries of the feminine mind'. Once we were dancing together at a party. Danny pressed me close and murmured: 'I've wanted you since the first time I saw you.' I lurched backwards and knocked against a harpsichord, upsetting a glass of wine into its valuable, exposed entrails. Half-flattered, I coyly smiled, feeling at the same time obscurely patronised. Yet I myself inwardly patronised Danny for her lack of cool.

Danny, like Jos and Percy and Maurice, responded to me-as-Writer in terms of herself, not of me. It was as if to be a Writer were some male preserve. Danny was different from the others only in being more unequivocally male. That her status as Writer had proven reality gave her a far stronger identity–hers was no subjective pose. Why then did she need to emphasise my femininity?

The identity Writer, intended as a measure of my sophistication, exposed my naivety. I had never seen being-a-Writer as having anything to do with gender–why should it? There were lots of women writers. Yet the wish to talk about writing seemed invariably to lead to heavy-handed flirtation or at least to general awkwardness about my sexual status. I couldn't understand it.

Perhaps they thought I lacked talent and had not the courage, or nastiness, to say so. The presence or absence of talent was certainly another source of unease. Danny, and others, seemed to assume that an Artist was someone especially gifted, or at least qualitatively different from other people. They seemed to see talent as some rare property. In their eyes the Artist was like the child in the advertisement for instant porridge–magically glowing, his body surrounded by a phosphorescent halo.

Percy did not see it like that. His view of writing as a craft to be learned was healthier and less pretentious by far, but did not amount to an Identity. If to be a Writer was *not* something special, how could it be an Identity? If it were not a destiny, then it became simply another kind of work–work undertaken in an unrelenting solitude. This solitude did not offer me the affirmation of the mirror. In the solitude of my hours as Writer I was oppressed by a huge, light emptiness which my identity was too insubstantial to fill. Yet I sought in writing for an inner self, not recognising that it would be in projects, in activities, in relationships and, it must be admitted, in the acquisition of possessions that a sense of identity would reside.

I was preoccupied with my solitude. I read novels about the ultimate solitude of the individual reduced to his own core by the pressures of an extreme situation–alone, in a prison cell, facing torture perhaps. I read books about brainwashing, and accounts of their sufferings by the survivors of concentration camps and resistance movements. These prison cell books asked: how does the prisoner manage to survive this solitude? Sometimes, it seemed, he did not. Perhaps no core of identity existed. Others, defined as 'enemy', 'terrorist', 'guerilla', 'Jew' or 'communist' by their gaolers found strength and identity in these very definitions: 'They called me a terrorist, a gangster—I always remembered that I was a revolutionary.' How weak of me, then, that I lacked the will to assert my identity against the unwelcome counter-definitions that pressed in on me.

But my identity as a would-be Writer warred with my other identities, as intellectual, as social worker, as dandy, as well-adjusted gay. As an intellectual I thought so much about the nature of the novel and the process of writing it that I called the whole enterprise into question. I read with anxious envy the new novels by young women that seemed to appear almost weekly. Here were the Young Girls again, their youthful subjectivity transformed into a clear and unequivocal 'truth'. They were all innocence and certainty. They had none of my doubts. I got no pleasure from writing but was bogged down in the stickily solemn longing to have something worthwhile to say.

I was preoccupied with the relationship of fiction to reality, and dashed by the recognition that the writers I admired had some kind of magic, a sleight of hand that turned dull life into a vision of beauty. Our expedition to Illiers proved as much. In this village near Paris, Proust had spent the summers of his childhood. My lover and I, with a friend, set off in the expectation that Proust's novel was about to open out before our very eyes. We stepped down off the train into flat, grey streets, our high spirits already evaporating. We trudged through a dismal, lifeless village with a bleak church. At length we found the house in which Proust had stayed. We knocked on the door. After a long wait we heard shuffling footsteps in slow progress towards the door. An ancient, wavering Frenchman stared at us. His papery skin, mauve lips and watering eyes made him look very ill. Wonderfully polite, he explained that his health made him hesitant to show us round. However, as sincere 'jeunes Proustiens' . . . All at once a claw-like hand with blood-red nails appeared and began to drag him away from the door. 'You will kill an old man,' screamed a haggard but much younger woman, her straggling grey locks falling over a face distorted with passion, 'I have to keep them away from him–they will kill him–what are you trying to do, vultures and murderers!' 'But my dear they are only young Proustians–they have come from far away' he turned vaguely to us–'vous n'êtes pas de la région?' Our friend smiled, flattered to have been mistaken for a Frenchman, even if from some other part of the country. The old man was now being slowly but inexorably dragged away from the doorway, protesting feebly: 'But my dear, they are sincere . . . we should not turn them away . . .' But the door was slammed in our faces.

Somewhat stunned by this incident, we turned disconsolately to our map and tried to work out how to follow the two famous 'walks' taken by Proust in his childhood. These walks had immense symbolic significance in Proust's novel as revelations both of beauty and of various social and philosophical truths. Above all, the walks, which had appeared to the child to be in two entirely different directions, had proved, as he realised in adult life, eventually to join.

We started off on what we hoped would prove to be the shorter of these walks, along 'Swann's way'. It turned out to be much longer–and duller–than we had expected, excruciatingly boring in fact, and before long we had flung ourselves grumpily down on the grass verge and started to bicker as we looked across the flat, scrubby fields, feeling cheated by Proust himself. We began to think longingly of coffee, drinks, sandwiches. It seemed a long way back into the village and they grey sky began to look like rain. We found no café, and spent a long hour at the sleepy railway halt waiting for the train to take us back to Paris.

*

That was in 1963. By that time I was well established within my relationship with my lover. Unfortunately this relationship was itself in some ways at odds with my identity of Writer.

I had rejected marriage, yet entered into a marriage-like relationship with another woman. We became a gay couple. Our relationship was of the period–the period of respectable homophile movements and of political pressure for modest reform. We should never have dreamt of the slogan of 1970: 'We are the people our parents warned us against.' On the contrary we set out to prove that we were as nice, as ordinary, as stable and as normal as the straightest heterosexual couple. I felt the status of being single to be associated with loneliness, inadequacy and withdrawal. The single person had failed, was suffering almost from a form of social psychosis. But the gay couple made the statement that homosexuals too could love, could be well-adjusted.

Our enactment of responsible respectability, a sort of gay Fabianism, was hardly compatible with the persona of *femme damnée* I was so eager to adopt when I read Baudelaire's poetry, which promised me hells of insatiable sensation and the madness of impossible desires. My unrestrained romanticism made me feel most intensely alive when unhappily in love, yet I simultaneously longed to prove to the world that homosexuality and happiness were not necessarily mutually contradictory.

To live out a 'gay marriage' was to express a whole gamut of clashing meanings, statements, ideologies. I sought some kind of free identity in this assertion of originality and difference, only to find myself willy-nilly acting out the assumptions of the time. We simultaneously

80

denied and bore witness to marriage, to normality and to a domestic and companionate ideal cemented by the shared ownership of home and income, and symbolised by the social understanding that we were to be asked out together. We believed in the possibility of an open relationship, but enacted a solid respectability tolerated by society. We were honest with our friends about the nature of our relationship, but we never pulled the tail of the crouching tiger of prejudice.

However respectable this twin-like identity, which depended for its existence on another identity, one's 'other half', it caused problems at work, for at work, initially as a social work student, later in a hospital, even the most 'mature' gay brought a whiff of the Baudelairean into the interviewing room. My black leather coat caused raised eyebrows. I was too apt to be a dandy at work, while an intense Miss Wilson, psychiatric social worker, hovered at my elbow when I was trying to be a Writer or a *femme damnée* at play.

No aristocratic or dandified distance enhanced Miss Wilson's identity. Indeed I felt that as Miss Wilson, the psychiatric social worker, I expressed all the worst and most conflicting parts of 'my life'–whatever that was. And at work 'my life' felt like the endless refusal of things to be as I wanted them, and the refusal of others to grant me the identity I craved.

How could Miss Wilson relate to my socialism? I often felt it was frivolous and self-indulgent for me and my colleagues to dabble so obsessively in every nuance of a 'client's' emotional state, yet care so little about social conditions, although that was how we had been trained, a training that had not prepared me for the poverty in which my 'clients' lived. I had never seen such social conditions before. I ventured out from the great, dark portals of the hospital to the slums of the East End and Islington and Hackney, mile after mile of waste and desolation. The houses and sometimes the inmates themselves decayed like rotten teeth. Sometimes the walls seemed to be kept in place only by the dirt that caked them together, sometimes the human beings held in one piece by the clothing that bundled them up. I did not only see poor people, but it was the poor that I remembered. Not that I was inspired to action—I merely froze again, this time from a sense of impotence. My shiny new identity, Miss Wilson the social worker, seemed shrill and tinny in the midst of this depressed squalor. I could tell that the broken men and women—mostly women—I visited expected nothing from me or from life. They huddled into their poverty or sickness, hoping that the grey rags of it might keep out the worst of the cold. They were patient, quiet—as if anxious not to rouse the tiger of wrath.

Death—the hospital was dark with it. Since the night when my mother had taken me with her on her visit to my dying grandfather, I had associated hospitals with death. Once there was someone's life blood all over the tiled floor in the Out-patients. In our cramped department I learned of insidious, terrifying illnesses, tumours of the brain, wasting of the nerves, slow death of the senile, sudden death of the young.

It would never do to write about all this. It did not occur to me. I could not have written about it without acknowledging my fear. But I buried my fear, although it lay somewhere at the core, part of some negated, deep identity. I fled into my escapist identities. 'The very heart of me,' throbbed one of the juke box numbers at the gay club—and that meant love affairs, didn't it?

*

The night before Christmas Eve our flat was empty, nothing left on the bare boards but a bed and an electric fire for the new tenant. She—her name was Hazel—seemed desolate with nothing but the bed and the fire. We made love all night in the empty room. It was the beginning of a sad, passionate love affair, the beginning of a triangle, source of drama and of loving cruelties, of guilt, selfishness and the 'failure to connect', all masked as moral puzzles, brain teasers to which the correct solution might always be found round the next corner.

*

We meanwhile, the perfect couple (and can't the perfect couple always accommodate a third?), moved to the Midlands. Provincial life might be the setting for a novel, but I was deterred by the thought that it had all been done before. There was a dampness in the air. The university campus was up on a hill. None of the townspeople seemed to know where it was. I liked the seedy, melancholic languor of the town, where eighteenth-century terraces backed onto a canal, and the redbrick factories stood foursquare in the Victorian dignity of their neo-Roman style.

The testimony of our first landlady may stand for the working-class lives packed together in the solid, industrial city and spreading with the suburbs and the arterial roads and the inter-war council estates out towards the old villages in the clefts of the green hills. A pale, plump woman, she used to read the *News of the World* while we ate our Sunday breakfast. The tabloid scandals evoked her own past:

'Look at that—he's left his wife and gone off with her. Yes—now I say a woman can take *any* man away from his family ... You haven't to judge a man always by what he does. Sometimes a man gets so tangled with another woman that he can't get away ... he can't get back ...

'It was a woman like that came between me and my husband. When I was young, mind you, I had a lot of young men around me, but I never had eyes for any one of them but Jack. I used to sit upstairs night after night and listen for his footsteps and I got so I could recognise his footsteps from among all the other men walking home. Well, then of course the time came he'd to go to the war to fight–the First World War, this was, you know, not the last one–and still I used to sit upstairs every evening, and crying my eyes out because his footsteps didn't come past. I couldn't get out of the way of expecting to hear them, and yet at the same time I was sure he'd never come back.

'But he did come back. And we were married. I'd set my heart on it, I was that stupid in love with him. And they were terrible hard times then, oh terribly hard, right after we were married. We rented a little house–it only cost 7s/6d [about 37p] a week in those days, but of course there was no bath nor nothing like that, and then, no sooner than I found I was in the family way but my husband he caught double pneumonia, it was that cold on the building sites, he was a builder you see. So that lost him his job, and I had to find some work to do.

'Well–I went back to the laundry where I'd worked before I was married, the woman who ran it, she liked me because I was always a good worker. But I was so silly proud, I didn't want the neighbours to know–so I used to slip out of an evening and get the washing and bring it back in a basket and do it at home late at night. I used to get a shilling [5p] for a pair of sheets and I could make about ten shillings [50p] a week that way. And that was a lot in those days . . .

'After my husband came out the hospital I nursed him at home a long while–and he got that dejected with no money coming in but his sick benefit, he did get that–it didn't come to above ten shillings–and then there was what I earned. And there was coals to get, a terrible hard winter we had that time after he were ill. And there was no work in the building trade, nothing at all. There was ice and snow everywhere. And there was the baby to feed as well.

'So in a bit I took another job, waiting in a café–I'd go out from six till half past ten each night and serve the suppers, and I enjoyed that–setting the tables with the red and white gingham cloths they had, and talking to the customers, it was a bit of life, you see.

'Then in the spring they had a new buildings works out above the town, and my husband got work there. So I asked a little girl from down the road to come in–I'd give her a supper and a sixpence and I knew she was glad of that because they were a big family and terribly poor. Seven or eight of those children there were–and you know sometimes all they had to eat of an evening was potatoes, and they'd sit huddled round the fire, the lot of them, and bake the potatoes in the coals and eat them with dripping and salt and pepper. You know sometimes I think people don't know what the life of the poor people was in those days. And yet though it was so terribly hard, I don't mean it was all sorrow and suffering–I think the poor people really knew how to enjoy themselves in those days. People got their enjoyment from little things then, you know–if you're young and poor too you really taste your pleasures, everything tastes stronger, pleasure and pain alike.

'But the little thing's mother fell ill, and so she couldn't come to see after the baby for me any more. So one day I was in the little shop on the corner, and the daughter of the man as ran it: "Why, I wouldn't mind coming in for the evening," she said. So that's what we did.

'Now this girl Nancy, she wasn't a beautiful girl at all– but she had a good job–she'd got on, you see, and she always dressed herself nicely, and she was slim, quite a tall girl, a quiet sort of person too. I liked her well enough. And so it went, for some time.

'Well then, one day I met a woman lived further up the road: "You don't look well, Emmy," she said. "I think you're daft, I do, working yourself to the bone, and you know you're no sooner out that door of a night but your husband's inside with that Nancy."

'And I was mad, I was that *furious*, I told her what I thought of her–put a brave face on it, you see, though I was

85

that upset underneath, I didn't know what to do. It tormented me, it did, I was that stupid about him, oh I thought the world of him–and all those hard times we'd been through together. So I kept quiet a long time.

'And then one day his uncle that had moved to London wrote and said to him to come down and join him–there was more work in the South, and better pay. I was ready to weep, because in those days London was a long way off–it was like a foreign country almost, it wasn't just a hop on a train. But he said he must go. And by that time–well, there was something unspoken between us. And then the night before he left, he said: "I won't be coming back Emmy. But I'll write, and send you money." And I said: "It's Nancy, isn't it?" And he said: "Yes." And after that neither of us said a word–as if we were turned to stone.

'I struggled on somehow, though I heard nothing of him for months. But people were starting to talk about Nancy, she got bigger you see. And one evening I heard a knock at the door, and when I opened it, there she was. Oh, she might have been a ghost, she looked that pale. And she leant against the doorpost and said to me: "I got rid of it, Emmy, it's gone."

'I brought her in, of course, right away, and I gave her a cup of tea and a warm by the fire: "I've a friend told me where to go," she said, "I went to see this woman, out on the London Road, she does that sort of thing. But I never told her I was seven months gone–so she brought it away for me. But, oh Emmy, it was alive, it cried out, just the once, so the old woman laid it on its face to smother it, and then she threw it on the fire under the copper."

'And I thought–he should never have let her do that. So I said as I'd write to him, and I'd give him the divorce. And then she started to bleed again, and I had to run for the doctor.

'He came back after he got my letter, and he went to live with Nancy. There was many that wouldn't speak to her, but–well where's the point in that? And in the end I got my divorce–that was the poor people's divorce they had in those days, they asked all these questions. But do you know, he *wouldn't* get married to her. He wouldn't. Two children they had as well. He used to come round and see me, now and again, and he'd beg me to have him back. But I didn't feel the same to him any more.

'And in the end he did marry her. And my two used to go round there to play with the babies or bring them back here; and so the thing was patched up after a fashion. And when I saw Nancy in the street or the shop we'd pass the time of day quite comfortably.

'And then he died. Still quite young he was. He was fixing some slates on a roof, and there was a terrible wind got up, and it blew his ladder right away from the side of the house, you see, and he fell off and was killed straight-way. I went to the funeral of course. We sat side by side, she and I.

'I'd married again by then. My second husband, he's a good man, we're happy enough, but I say you never really love a man like that but the once. And when it's gone it's gone forever.'

Her story demonstrated some rootedness I lacked. How could I write when whole tracts of experience eluded me, when I hadn't lived? It was 1964–then it was 1965–then 1966–and still I was searching for what I could do and be in life, held back by a sense of imprisonment within my class and within some stifling, artificial prison of gender.

A force named Social Mobility had swept us up and let us fall in this, one of the many encampments of nomads in the university towns of Britain, for academics seemed like a new wandering tribe of strangers in their own land. We moved to a house full of university people, and partook of a hedonistic lifestyle. We became part of a group that was always changing, yet always the same, progressing in circles rather than a straight line. However much the personnel of the group might change, the group itself could not die, but had its own existence, or so it seemed at one time.

A hedonistic lifestyle in the mid sixties meant rich food, alcohol, heterosexual affairs. Social life was elaborate and time-consuming, and some members in particular of this loosely cohesive, tolerant social group had a gift for turning what was essentially an aimless round of drinking, dining out, talking and womanising into a series of Occasions. We never just went drinking. We went to sample a special malt whisky at a pub someone had discovered, or to play bar billiards thirty miles out of town because that was the only pub in the county with a bar billiards table. Pleasure was taken seriously. The group elevated pleasure into a moral system. There were many large dinner parties, and they grew more and more ambitious. There was the Indian dinner party, when we spent a day beforehand chopping onions and grating raw ginger, our hands and eyes red and stinging by the end. There were innumerable Middle Eastern dinners, and traditional English roast dinners as well. (One of these was cooked by me for a visiting external examiner: 'Delicious–what a pity you're not married, my dear,' he said.)

Then there was the sucking pig dinner–perhaps the most successful of all. Days were spent organising it, and before it was taken to the baker's oven to be cooked, we all gathered round to admire the pig as it lay on its roasting dish. It looked rather pathetic, hairless and pink, with its trotters outstretched and a tasteful strip of liver arranged down its snout to conceal the bullet mark. It was almost like the awesome, sacred centre of some ritual–a burnt offering to our hedonism. I'd never seen a sucking pig before. It looked rather like a dog.

The following year there was a whole lamb dinner. Before the lamb we were to have halibut kebabs, charcoal-grilled in the back garden, and served with Hollandaise sauce. Unfortunately a downpour drenched the grill and the sauce curdled. It was on this occasion that I began to wonder seriously if too much of a fuss were not being made about pleasure. A whole day was spent at the wrong end of the group will to pleasure. Ordered to move furniture, chop vegetables and mix salad dressing, I became openly rebellious, feeling more and more like a naughty school child, and spoilt the fun by refusing to care ardently whether the strawberries were served with cream or with red wine.

By the period of the final, roast beef dinner, the whole atmosphere of hedonism had somehow soured. The side of beef was almost raw, and no one ate the chocolate gateau I'd made. The evening ended in a complex scene, as someone's neglected wife slapped the face of a man who made a pass at her, while her husband quarrelled with his mistress, and my lover and I left in fury at the rejection of the gateau.

Despite what the sociologists half jokingly referred to as 'our very privatised, bourgeois existence' the group also hung together on the basis of its members being left-wing radicals. There was a more serious, political side to life. Our friends campaigned around issues of racial equality. We went into the Asian community and got the immigrants to register as voters. And here again was another life more authentic than my own. There was the ceremony of the Sikh temple. There was the Indian workers' leader, who said of his fellow countrymen: 'They think they will go back to their villages, but they will never go back. They cannot go back.' And he described the vast plains, the peasant villages, the compulsion to escape. We white women sat uncomfortably with the men and the Asian wives served us with refreshments.

There were also two general elections and much campaigning for Harold Wilson and the Labour Party. It wasn't exactly the dawn of a new era, but things were looking up.

Ironically, it was in this permissive environment that the Perfect Couple began to come under strain. We were 'accepted' weren't we?–but neither we nor our friends knew quite what acceptance meant. To be different might in the beginning have seemed daring to me–but here it was an emptiness, a series of negations. I was negated sexually. Either I was not sexy because I was a lesbian, or I was a lesbian because I was not sexy. I was outside the main swing of things, which was–or felt as if it was–the ring'o'roses of the heterosexual whirl. Work roles contributed to my unease. The group tended to define my lover as masculine because she worked with men, had a job with masculine status. My position was ambiguous. I busied myself with interior decoration and cookery, but not because I wished to be a housewife. My place was not with the girlfriends and the wives–or was it? Yet I didn't belong with the men. So I often felt threatened by a kind of social extinction. I was a nothingness, neither masculine nor feminine. In this milieu I felt it would have been too uncool to talk about being a Writer–I was just effeminate, a dandy. My preoccupation with style and sensation declined into a kind of camp stance to life. Without realising it, I was unhappy.

Seven

To return to an earlier period, it was in 1961 that I first saw the inside of a mental hospital. The old Victorian asylum was situated on the far edge of London, whose flowery suburbs had crept towards it to encircle it in the 1920s. The grounds still fostered an illusion that you were in the countryside, and the redbrick palace with its wings, courts and turrets, imposed a spiritual and romantic atmosphere. In the drugged peace of the shrubberies sat someone who might be an aunt or a retired nanny. Only when you drew close did her muttering, her pudding-basin haircut, wrinkled stockings and blood-boltered lipstick strike a strange note. She was like a child's caricature of a person, carelessly chalked in. Solitaries paced the gravel sweep of the drive, passing one another with no sign of recognition. A country house with a difference—only at first glance could you have mistaken it for hotel or stately home.

To walk in the endless corridors was to be plunged in a deep-sea nightmare. Men and women shuffled past— shoals of deadpan fishes in the aquatic half light. Pasty-skinned, they wore shrunken, heavy clothes. They chewed over a few words, over and over, so that language, food of the self, was reduced to a wad of wornout chewing gum. They smoked and smoked until their finger tips looked like fag ends, stained sepia with nicotine. And always present was the smell of urine mingling with disinfectant, a sweet and sour, subliminal reminder of incontinence, of something shameful that was only half hidden.

The corridors led to the back wards. And there was the Silence. When sun poured through the windows it varnished the long room, catching the silent figures in its sticky amber so that they moved as if swimming through glue. Eyes bewildered, or shuttered and blank–a confused chattering of anger quickly hushed–sometimes there was a gleam of malicious life. But nothing ever happened, and no one was even waiting for anything to happen. And yet there was always the fear, because there was always the Silence. Madness downgraded to nursery naughtiness–mad women with socks and bows in their hair–did nothing to lessen the horror of the Silence, a placid and banal horror.

A horror because time did not pass. We were all caught in a gap between one moment and the next. We were all holding our breath. And I knew, and the nurses knew, and *they*–the ghosts–knew that beneath that heavy lid of silence was a great roar of sound, an endless scream of rage and pain on which the stone lid had been ruthlessly slammed down.

I was sane, of course. I was a student social worker. And the Silence reinforced the sanity of myself and the other functionaries, as we swopped jokes in the canteen, or skirted patients in the corridors. I dumbly registered the terror, and saw that some of the sights were obscene, but I did not protest, nor see how the Silence could be broken. And I recognised the fascination with which we, the sane ones, lived cheek by jowl with the mad, yet totally cut off from them. The closeness of those lost ones, swallowed up in that crack in time, gave our identities strength. Or did it? Here also, even here, was a sense of a life more raw and more extreme. They dared at least to be mad.

*

How did I first get to hear about Freud? Everyone has always already heard of him.

My parents had read avidly when they were Out in the Tropics. My mother had read Gibbon's *Decline and Fall of the Roman Empire* as she sustained the British one; my father had read Havelock Ellis and Freud, writers to whom he referred with a knowing air of offended morality. These writers (like Somerset Maugham, who had done even worse in betraying the dark secrets of the Empire settlers and administrators) had said things that should not have been said, better never mentioned, but clearly once set down in print, irresistible.

I had heard of Paul (who was later to relieve me of my virginity) and his green carnation while still at school. Paul's father was a psychoanalyst, and Paul's utterances on the subject of psychoanalysis had been repeated to me by Jenny, the Diana Dors of my Oxford days. In the public library I found some volumes of Freud. These case histories read like a book of short stories and should have been called *Tales of Old Vienna.* There were family dramas and mysteries, stories of love gone wrong, of misunderstandings, of partings and reunions, adultery and untimely death. Servants played an important role in these tales, as the bearers of illicit knowledge or pleasure, or both. They were the outsiders in these family dramas. I read these novellas, inwardly visualising them against the background of a Dutch impressionist painting I had seen at the Tate Gallery, 'Boulevard de Clichy under Snow'. That was how I imagined Vienna, with wintry streets, horse-drawn cabs, ladies with bustles and men in top hats. It was the world of Proust again. Yet, unlike Proust, the reading of these tales brought a feeling of frustration and disappointment, since after its initial promise each would drift off into strange byways, into back alleys of the imagination where odd physical details and mental tics became the focus of the author's attention. Yet they still caught my imagination because of their promise (even if this was never fulfilled) that they would open a door into myself. It was as if I might one day turn the page and find my own story written there, the explanation of my feelings.

When it came, seven or eight years later, to a question of training, I was drawn to psychiatry by this hope of self-knowledge rather than by a desire to help others. Or at least I imagined an expansion and a liberation of the self in the acquisition of an understanding that could be used to help others. It was 1961, the year I bought the typewriter.

I was to train as a psychiatric social worker, and my training was committed to a psychoanalytic outlook. Psychoanalysis was certainly not just a cure, nor was my training simply a training in techniques and a theory. Psychoanalysis was a special and privileged world. The training offered me an entry to it.

We had, we felt, a radical critique of the psychiatry practised in the mental hospitals, of the 'disease model' of psychiatry. Mental disturbance, we believed, was not an illness, but represented the acting out of emotional conflicts going back to childhood days. These could be understood and unravelled by means of the 'talking cure', that is by encouraging patients to talk about their problems, their unhappiness, their fantasies, their past. We were careful to distinguish ourselves from therapists, yet we did use a modified version of psychoanalytic techniques. But there was a confusion because in practice we were not trying to cure the schizophrenics, the seriously estranged from life, but rather their families, or whole other 'client' groups. 'It helps to be listened to,' we said, as they told us their stories of poverty, social neglect or crime. And while we did not believe they were 'ill' in an organic sense, we did refer to their behaviour as 'immature' or 'pathological', as deviating from a subtle norm of 'mental health'. In the end psychoanalysis too set up a barrier between the mad and the sane.

From the threshold at which I hesitated, the privileged world of psychoanalysis opened out as a civilised domain where beauty and quietude were prized above all else. The inhabitants of this world valued art and music, 'Western Civilisation' valued the ordered and the composed, the peace of traditional relationships and their stability in the face of the disorder and wildness expressed by those on whom my training was to be used. It was not that anyone denied the existence of the tigers of wrath. But our task in life was to tame them. I was offered the choice between two roles. Either I must be a deviant, acting out in mess and stridency my unresolved, childish conflicts, or I could be one of the Mature Ones, those calm, vaguely parental figures who had left excess of emotion behind them and gazed at me, and at everyone, always with a look of pained and patient understanding. Their eyes and brows drawn downwards in sorrow at the foolish sins of their patients, they allowed a restrained sweetness to curve their lips as they spoke their seemingly tentative 'insights': 'I expect you are feeling upset . . .,' 'You seem to be feeling angry . . .' And for them there was always something questionable about anger.

Clients and patients were often judged to be regrettably 'angry' about their poverty, generally miserable material circumstances, unpleasant spouses and difficult children. I learned that it would be a mistake to be sidetracked by these surface difficulties. Feelings, after all, are more important. Surely only a philistine would rate material well-being above a bouquet of refined and sensitive feelings? I thought of Fairlawns, and of the children there who had been in care because of poverty, because their parents were homeless, unemployed, ill or widowed. I remembered too the things that had been said there about social workers and psychiatrists, the sharp scepticism towards middle-class patronage.

I had, all the same, imagined the psychoanalyst as a romantic figure. The analyst of my imagination was both threatening and attractive, no dowdy bourgeois, but more of a Svengali. Alone, of those with whom I came in contact, a famous psychoanalyst who lectured to us each week about his work with children seemed something of a magician. His gift for dramatisation turned dry case histories into genuine 'romances' of family life and personal liberation.

Even he, though, like the rest, endorsed the conventional

morality that institutional psychoanalysis upheld. I had been drawn to psychoanalysis by its promise of revelations of the unconscious and the liberation that this had appeared to involve. It had, at first acquaintance, seemed subversive with its exploration of sexuality and eroticism. Now I found myself entangled in something closer to a moral hygiene movement, an ideology that elevated the family uncritically and seemed concerned to understand the subversion of the unconscious only in order to cage it. Freud had claimed, hadn't he, only to cure his patients of their 'hysterical misery' so that they could get on with their lot of 'common human unhappiness'. These doctors and social workers claimed far more. For them, a conventional family life was the only source of real happiness ('maturity').

My fellow students, too, endorsed this glorification of the family. No matter that their family lives seemed in some cases harassed and unrewarding, while many of them were indeed unmarried. Dave, for example–as I look back he seems to stand as epitome of all those anxious, authoritarian men, who felt it so important to tell me how wonderful it was to be a woman. Dave, engrossed in the work of Melanie Klein, never tired of repeating to me that the organising psychological principle of the world was male envy of women's capacity to bear and suckle children. This was then used to justify the exclusion of women from paid work, for what work could possibly be as worthwhile and as valuable as the joy of creating and rearing a child. Why, in that case, did men like Dave not spend more time on child-rearing themselves? What I most powerfully sensed, unspoken, was his hostility to women, his denigration, his general irritation with his wife, who, sitting about all day at home and having a hard time with her baby, aroused simply his impatience. And although he glorified motherhood in the abstract, it was clear that nothing could have induced him to stay at home.

I smiled, silently cynical about the Dave syndrome. Yet

morally I was isolated. I experienced a faint, knowing disapproval if I ever questioned the position of women, and this made me feel rejected, and uncertain of myself. Had I intended to denigrate maternity? Was it true, as one woman student said, that women only became lesbians if they were sexually unattractive? The famous child analyst said almost carelessly, in passing, as it were, that on the one hand lesbianism was only a form of mother-child relationship, on the other that homosexuality between men involved 'a lot of killing'–all homosexuals dismissed in a sentence as either babies or sadistic. Was my life so inauthentic? Ironically, although I'd given little thought to the possibility of motherhood for myself, I definitely did not think of myself as a 'career woman'; in fact I disliked that label.

And my self doubt was only compounded because I was a 'bright girl' on my course, one of the youngest, a bright, precocious little girl, perceptive *and* brainy, although it was not officially admitted that you could be both intellectually sharp and emotionally 'in touch'. On the contrary, a subtle antagonism was set up between intellect and feeling. You were 'intellectualising' when you raised logical or philosophical objections to the Freudian canon. I was told that after all it was possible to be *too* clever. You can't prove everything. Above all, although this was not spelt out in so many words, it was unwomanly to be too intellectual. This too was puzzling, since again Freud himself had not set up an opposition between thought and feeling. On the contrary he had argued for the more conscious and rational control of and access to feeling, for co-operation between emotions and rationality.

The attitudes of those amongst whom I found myself were unacceptable to me, as was their complacency in these reassuring doctrines, and often, I felt, their hypocrisy. Almost all my peers and teachers appeared to endorse conservative moral, intellectual and political attitudes.

Anything else was explained away as the end product of emotional immaturity. To rebel was always to flout the internalised father. To challenge paternalistic wisdom was always to act out the infant in oneself. One set of attitudes alone denoted maturity. The rest reflected a state of arrested development.

I was silent. I stifled my anger. I knew, after all, that my anti-conventional stance was sometimes adolescent and silly. But I also knew that that did not make conservatism *right*, either. My only form of defence was to nurse my scepticism in secret. But my outrage was stifled not because I should have caused trouble for myself had I flouted the fundamental beliefs of my teachers, but because after all psychoanalysis *did* fascinate me. I was by no means immune to its power.

I was drawn to the world of psychoanalysis when I interviewed patients, entered with them into the charmed world of secret understanding and experienced the delight of revealing an individual to him or herself. This was to make a pattern out of the seeming senselessness or dreariness of tired lives, of suffering, of wasted opportunities. Each week the group of psychoanalysts, psychologists and social workers sat in conference. A case was discussed. A decision was made. These workers, dedicated, patient, sombre yet sensitive, anatomised unconscious emotions and laid them out clear, translated into a pattern, so that it all had meaning. To give to patients the meaning of their lives seemed a delicate and admirable task: 'It was like having a light turned on in a dark room,' said one grateful patient by way of farewell to the social worker who had talked to her three times a week for three years.

The case conference should have been painted in the manner of Rembrandt's 'The Anatomy Lesson', with the therapists posed as if dissecting a psyche instead of a corpse. Fantasy, hatred and sexual passion, incest and parricide, flared and flickered within the circle around the conference room table. Perhaps it was more like one of those Magritte paintings–a rather dead seascape or room transformed by a brass instrument which rests on the sand or hangs in mid-air, unaccountably in flames.

I should, too, have liked to have my own Analyst, someone who would reveal me to myself. I had a persistent image of a wood or walled garden in which were locked the secrets of my emotions. I read many times an introductory work on Melanie Klein in which a similar image had persisted in the analysis of one particular patient. In her fantasies her parents were locked together, beak to beak like two birds, in some frigid embrace in an enclosed garden. Somehow for the patient herself it was necessary to break out from this locked place emotionally. The secret garden was also the place at the heart of a larger tangled garden or wood where the Minotaur-Analyst awaited the seeker after truth. In my mind I held an image of an Edwardian illustration by Edmund Dulac of etiolated romantic figures against darkly picturesque trees and trailing undergrowth. I remembered also the children's novel, *The Secret Garden,* in which the child heroine, abandoned in India when her parents have died of plague, finds in her new, strange, English home a secret garden where she meets and plays with a mysterious little boy who suffers from some lingering illness. The magic of the secret garden in the end heals both his physical delicacy and her grief and loneliness.

The secret garden was walled, overgrown, forgotten, locked in a peaceful yet eerie daydream. It was a Victorian image linked to two companion images; of Mariana in the Moated Grange, a woman imprisoned by a lost love in a forgotten and neglected place, and of the Lady of Shalott who, psychologically imprisoned in her room, saw life only through a mirror. The secret garden was a contradiction, for it was both a retreat and a journey's end, a goal. There was the world; and there was the secret life, related and

99

joined in the image of the neglected garden. Empty, silent, it was the image of lost joy that becomes a future hope, the transformation of nostalgia into a new desire.

But the price of entry was a high one. I should have had to make a religious leap in order to immerse myself in this new way of thinking. And this would have been dishonest, and untrue to the radical in me. So I stayed ambivalently on the threshhold.

Here, at the London School of Economics, as at Oxford, the hours when I felt least burdened by the problems of identity and commitment were those spent in the old library, rooms with yellow lighting and yellow oak panels and desks–sallow afternoons of dry yet pleasantly crowded loneliness. There, I immersed myself in psychology, looking for an alternative, never found, to psychoanalysis, lived in an interior world peopled with character types–introverts, extroverts, oral, anal, phallic characters, types dominated by the senses, the intellect or the intuition. They were, I felt, extraordinarily similar to the medieval astrological character types I'd studied at Oxford.

Then there were Kretschmer and Sheldon, who had classified personality according to bodily type: asthenic, athletic or pyknic, endomorphic, mesomorphic or ecto-morphic. I longed to be asthenic or ectomorphic, their names for the thin, artistic type. I hoped I was not a pyknic (stubby) or a soft, spherical endomorph. Eventually I decided I was a pyknic with ectomorphic limbs–a freak in other words, like a spider or an orang-utan.

There were yet other psychologists who described personality in terms of shopping lists of 'traits', character-istics that could be measured by tests and questionnaires. I answered all these in hopeful expectation. I owned well-thumbed Pelican editions of popular works in this line, and, finding one of these again recently was surprised by the answers I'd pencilled in in 1962. Did I really suffer from so many 'neurotic' symptoms, from headaches, dizziness, paranoid and schizoid feelings? Did I really care so much about censorship and so little about politics? Did I *really* believe that Communists and fascists were 'the same'?

Later–this was 1965–I visited an American woman in a vicarage in the East Anglian fens. She was researching into lesbian character types, and administered a Rorschach test to me in a room full of tennis trophies–won by her, I imagined, in some former life, these were the leftovers from some former identity. I enjoyed the opportunity to free-associate to the red and black and coloured 'ink blots'. Afterwards I looked up the answers in a book–and felt cheated again by the broken promises of psychology. Psychology never told you quite what you wanted to know.

I really preferred the medieval signs of the Zodiac. But could I live up to the image of Leo, my star sign? I lacked the bravura, the panache, the glamour. Surely no Leo was ever a social worker.

*

Four years passed. Sometimes I was transiently but overpoweringly unhappy in my 'couple' when a romance blew up on the side and opened out areas of myself that seem unexpressed and unfulfilled. At other times I felt an irritation that drove me to the point of screaming frustration because as a social worker I developed and expressed only one side of myself, felt intellectually unstimulated, felt often that I was acting, despite myself, against the interests of those who came to me for help, felt impotent and powerless. The possibility of going to a therapist was always held out tantalisingly, but my teachers had said to me: 'You don't go into analysis unless you're driven to it.'

Such a moment came. Or perhaps I created it. For a time I was possessed by an awful secret discontent. The Perfect Couple no longer seemed enough. The romance with the Third, with Hazel, wove into and out of our lives, then into it again. But that too was not enough. I longed to stop going against the grain, longed to cave in, to earn social approval instead of the dubious tolerance, the half-acceptance of our life in the provinces. Was I not as constrained by the Couple as I should have been by marriage, yet with none of the benefits? It began to seem too exhausting to swim against the tide. It began also to seem arrogant. Why should I have imagined that I was 'different' from all other women? My 'identity' could, after all, be created only with the help of a man.

But the man to whom, without really admitting it to myself, I assigned the role of saviour, rejected me. Hysterical because I felt I was being denied even the identity of 'ordinary woman', I returned to London and my first search for therapy began.

One psychoanalyst told me that I didn't seem very interested in self-understanding—which I interpreted as another humiliating rejection. An old and distinguished analyst seemed angry with me right through the interview, and kept warning me that unless I took action, I was going to miss the last train to heterosexuality. A pink Pigling Bland with a boudoir in Hampstead listened to my story—which was beginning to bore me—and told me I was very sick. A young, handsome analyst brought us back to the permissive sixties: 'After all, we're all more or less bisexual.' At least he talked to me as one sophisticate to another.

But the experience of warring diagnoses was far from reassuring. I made a final sortie into West End consulting rooms and enrolled myself in a therapeutic group. It was 1967. I wore a daffodil yellow coat which showed my thighs, with pale tights, patent leather strapped shoes and short, fringed hair, bobbed—'she breaks just like a little girl,' jeered Bob Dylan and the harsh music.

We—the Perfect Couple—were buying a house. When I talked about this in the group the analyst said it was male to think so much about money. He made it clear that he found me unfeminine: 'Why can't you be responsive,' he nagged, 'why can't you just wait and let someone love you–it's so much more womanly.' There was a high turnover in the group. The up and down seasick swing of love affairs like the big swings at a fair (was that what they meant by swinging?) claimed my attention, and I too left the group, turning against psychoanalysis once more in the wake of this unhelpful experience.

'We'–the couple, two people with a single shared identity–lived in a terrace of smart Islington cottages. There was a bright, jazzy side to my life, the paintbox clothes, the clubs, dinner parties, restaurants. The bright side was where I wasn't afraid. Going home on my own from a party I walked through Bayswater at three o'clock in the morning, without a care or a fear, with a 'fuck off' to kerb crawlers. Even at the depth of night in the metropolis, alone in empty streets, this was my daytime self and by day my self was the red, yellow, black and white of the decade, bright as a nursery school.

But there was the dark side. Did I love women or men or both? Each time an 'extra marital' relationship (not that there were many, but they often preoccupied me) swung from the high down to the sickening low I diagnosed myself depressed and turned back towards the neglected secret garden where I experienced my feelings, the irruptions of unwanted passions and moods of despair. I woke at three in the morning and froze in terror in the aftermath of dreams in which I was haunted by landscapes dark with despair in which women veiled in cobwebs waited for or wept away some departure. I was menaced by the irruption into these nightmares of terrifying figures–by a Victorian gentleman in a top hat and black clothes which changed–for some reason horrifically–to metallic blue, and by a woman with a hypo-dermic needle. Or there was a full-scale war in which I was shot dead, or in which, although the whole of London had been smashed with nuclear bombs, I was still running along the balcony of a block of flats as armed men closed in on me.

Strange to be more frightened in my own bed than in the empty streets at night. Why were my dreams so filled with fear? Why were they filled with the dusty classical paraphernalia of the Freudian pantheon, with phallic women, images of sadistic sexuality, punishment for unrecognised crimes, fear of the phallus, horror of death, universal disaster?

I was now working at the clinic at which I had trained at the other end of the sixties. I was still the Lady of Shalott who looked on the world through her mirror. There were student sit-ins. I visited the London School of Economics with another social worker from the clinic. The women's lavatories were covered with political graffiti. I'd never seen anything like it. When I came out of my cubicle my colleague was smoothing her hair, and wore the familiar pained look: 'It's the destruction to *property* that seems to dreadful.' I laughed, rudely. But when we talked about the graffiti at the clinic, the next day, we met disbelief: 'Women don't write graffiti,' one analyst explained kindly.

There was Vietnam. Even when I went on the great marches–as I'd once gone on CND marches–I was not really part of it but remained in some peculiar way a spectator. I was still passive, even if I was amongst the great concourse of the Good and the Just straggling endlessly across the worn mud of Hyde Park beneath the changeable grey sky.

At work I watched other lives through the mirror of my counselling sessions. The offices were comfortable. There was the material comfort of soft carpets, easy chairs and coffee and biscuits in the room where we sat between interviews, the clinic's social centre. I enjoyed the civilised mental comfort of our conversations, which twined themselves round the two great themes of Art and the Psyche. We constructed elaborate interpretations of a film, an exhibition of paintings, a TV documentary. There was always some symbolic meaning behind the meaning,

104

something more deeply personal in such works, a meaning that related them to general truths about the human soul. To interpret *is* a skill, and the discussions were always fascinating, creative, even poetic.

We also discussed patients–although full names were carefully avoided so that confidentiality was protected. The line was not always clear between clinical assessment and moral disapproval–there was a grey area in which the exploration of the unconscious and the reaffirmation of normative, conservative values became confused. There was a divide, too, between the therapists in this dark cocoon, and the bright fragments of patients' lives. *They* indulged in extra-marital affairs. The women had au pairs, or jobs, or–worse still–both, or were frigid, or hysterical, or castrating. The men were worldly, or too cynical, over-intellectual or too materialistic, unconsciously homo-sexual or emotionally impotent. The patients failed, in other words, as 'real' men or 'real' women. They enacted what the therapists–each seated attentively in sober suit or quiet dress-and-jacket–only observed.

I too had to pass judgment. At case conferences I was now the one who was expected to offer a role model to my students as I displayed my sensitive perceptions drawn from interviews in depth. I had a flair for sketching in these portraits and thereby contributing towards the assessments made by the Team. Regularly in this way I started to speak in public, even if only to groups of ten or twenty. I developed a confidence, even if only a confidence based on something I ultimately distrusted. I was supported by the Team, which also gave me confidence. The Team ran like a marriage. I arranged appointments, saw to the social side, the analyst took the male role of decision maker and ultimate authority. Like all conventional role-playing it had its charm. You reaped approval when you behaved like this. Yet this womanly role *was* ultimately unsatisfying, although paradoxically I did not mind being handmaiden to the doctor, in fact I rather enjoyed it. What irked me was that my work was always secondary. I had no professional autonomy.

Sometimes, therefore, I wondered about becoming a therapist myself. But I assumed from the start that this was a hopeless idea. I was too deviant, I would never be accepted. I had refused the womanly role. Yet after all, in the psychoanalytic world as a whole, if not in this particular clinic, there were plenty of women therapists who were 'unwomanly', who displayed an unrepentant masculinity or a strenuously unmarried lifestyle, or who, if married, combined their career with having a family. Yet it was often these women who expressed the most tradition-alist and conservative views on women's place. It was never they who were 'unfeminine' or 'bad mothers', yet they would readily judge other women as such.

A group of local women asked to talk to workers at the clinic about a community nursery they were trying to set up. This caused consternation. The head social worker was deputed to speak to them and to explain that the clinic was trying to help women to be *better* mothers (and by implication no woman who put her child in a nursery could be other than bad).

Then there was an insignificant incident which irritated me disproportionately. It was the discussion in a case conference about a mother who had failed an appointment. This woman had no money, had been deserted by her husband, had a daughter who didn't attend school, lived in a slum. When she finally managed to get to see me, she had an excuse for her previous missed appointment: 'Walking down the Malden Road, a wardrobe fell over on top of me.' My intention had been to present her sympathetically, but–as so often it seemed to me–the judgment of the case conference was–bad mother. They seemed blind to her threadbare poverty and her struggle to keep any sort of life going for herself and her child. And I thought of myself

106

when I had been a little girl, and of my own mother, driven anxiously here and there by poverty and abandonment. It was the old game of blaming the victim.

The sleek judgments angered me. It was in the end rich judging poor, bourgeoisie against workers. It was in the end as crude as that, behind the Chinese screen of art and sensitivity. The psychoanalysts travelled from consulting rooms and private practice to the prestigious temples of their wisdom, in closed cars, deeply and drainingly perceptive and at the same time blind.

These treacherous thoughts filled me with guilt. For after all they had given me confidence and had trusted me. And I repeatedly betrayed them with my doubts. Sometimes I argued in the coffee room—about trades unions, about student militancy—but if I said even one tenth of what I believed the consternation began to mount.

So my original feeling of ambivalence and hesitation gradually changed to a feeling of conflict, and that I was being actively pulled in two different directions. And there was a more fundamental problem now, in that my attitude towards Freud's own work became more critical. Once I had thought that the main problem was the interpreters of his theories. But the more I read the more it seemed to me that there were flaws and inconsistencies in his reasoning that could not be ignored. You did not have to insist on empirical evidence in order to see that his work was a tissue of brilliant insights, revolutionary suggestions, biologism, crude bourgeois pessimism, and pure speculation. But perhaps one could not judge it, intellectually, from the outside. Perhaps it was after all necessary to undergo the experience itself.

*

An intelligent woman of thirty-three, Fräulein Elisabeth von W introduced herself to me with the complaint that while she suffered from no particular neurotic symptoms, and professed herself free from

107

guilt although living in a homosexual relationship with another woman, the relationship itself no longer satisfied either partner and they were seeking an end to it. But it had proved difficult for them to part. At the same time, Fräulein von W admitted that although resident in the cosmopolitan city of Vienna she led what amounted to a double life. By day hers was a profession that has increasingly sought to assimilate itself to my own, for she was a practitioner in that branch of social work most closely associated with the practice of psychoanalytic therapy. Her social life by contrast was, not surprisingly, given her sexual predilections, passed within the *demi monde* of the 'homosexual community', respectable enough it is true, but nevertheless a part of her life whose existence could not be hinted at in the clinic where her working life was spent.

The task Fräulein von W set me was in essence a practical one. Could I assist her to separate from her companion? But I detected also the presence of external motives. In her working environment she lived and breathed an atmosphere of psychoanalysis. So, in seeking my help, she not only gained approval at work, where her sexual deviation, although a secret, caused a constant fear of a negative judgment on her character, but she also hoped, I surmised, to gain access to the inner secrets of the psychoanalytic world to which as a social worker she existed in a humble and peripheral relationship. She may even have dreamed at one time of herself training as an analyst.

It may be noted in passing–and we shall return to this point in our subsequent discussion of the case– that Fräulein von W did not altogether display a straightforward clinical picture. It would appear that since my death, or so they tell me, clear cut differentiations between neuroses and perversions have become somewhat clouded, and these replaced by a more prevalent type of what might be called character neurosis, such as that displayed by the patient in question. We may speculate to what extent these changes are related to changes in social custom in the direction of greater sexual freedom such as I myself formerly desired to see brought about. But these wider questions we must leave aside . . .

*

The house in St John's Wood was discreetly luxurious. I ran up the front steps on a sunny September day wearing a red-flowered Biba jacket hardly longer than my crotch-length skirt. A big-boned, smiling woman opened the door. It was *her*. As I followed her up some stairs I glimpsed through shiny white double doors a second, inner hall with parquet floor, console table, Persian rugs, a huge vase of flowers. That then was *her* secret life. Her consulting room was in another style, less luxurious, less pleasing, with stripped pine, Ercol chairs, Copenhagen ware, green plants. (And her husband's consulting room, sometimes glimpsed on the floor below, was in yet another style, heavy and masculine in black leather.)

I'd imagined that psychotherapy would help me to 'know myself' and that out of it would come a rounded picture of 'my personality'. But as in Freud's case histories, the 'self' was dissolved into incidents, en-counters, fleeting memories and all the rest of the detritus of life. I was not a 'personality' but the hollow centre of confused–and mostly boring–internal dramas.

My analyst, Mrs Z, made me describe endlessly the minutiae of my experience and memories. As these impressions and recollections of daily life crowded into my consciousness I was to let these lead me wandering into the Freudian back alleys of the past. Like a detective, Mrs Z picked through this rubbish basket of discarded events to look for leads and clues. She unravelled the surface appearance of consistency and reason with which I had attempted to construct myself and behind the surface uncovered not a 'self' but a space for the inter-play of violent, shapeless and amorphous emotions. There was a feeling of exhilaration and relief when a clue was deciphered and understood. So that's it! The simplicity of a sudden truth after all the scrabbling was refreshing, suddenly to *see* jealousy beneath the stereotyped image of a 'liberated' relationship, suddenly to *see* guilt crippling a generous impulse, or the spite behind an act of defiance. These were the moments of insight, the reward for all the work. But the twice or thrice weekly process of going through the rubbish was more often enervating, debilitating. It was no self indulgence to talk about oneself. It was a painful, dreary effort. Especially as I wandered back down the dusty infinite-regress corridors known as 'the past' a sense of boredom, or weariness, almost of nausea overtook me, against the slyness of my self-deceptions and the meanness of my emotions. Less than ever did I have a sense of my personality as willed and created. All was disintegrating panic, fear, anxiety, greed.

But at least one was to be precise about what exactly one's emotional response was at any given moment, so that these deceptions and meannesses should not so readily occur again. Nothing was to be glossed over with imprecise words. There was to be no generalisation. If I said: 'Well, I feel . . .,' Mrs Z pronounced with: 'Yes, but what *happened*?' She patiently pointed out time and again when I 'talked without saying anything'. Everything had to be concrete, accurate and not vague.

Yet occasionally a peculiar counter-current came. At certain moments the specific, satisfying interpretations gave way to the sonorous generalisations of theory. Then Mrs Z herself became vague or stereotyped: 'Could it be that ...' she would begin, so tentatively, and then would trundle out one of the clumsy old stage props–Oedipus, castration, penis envy–like a clumsy operatic moment when a 'god' descends from the flies on an all-too-visible wire.

These moments, the least satisfactory, were comparatively rare. In general, the analytic process seemed the opposite of an explanatory, synthesising or theorising one.

I no longer thought of Identity as a clearly outlined object. Now the self seemed more to resemble the representation of a monster in a fifties science fiction movie I watched on television at around this time. This 'thing from another world' was not represented directly on the screen. Instead, as audience one saw the world as the monster saw it through a huge, transparent bubble that was its eye. This bubble-eye clouded and distorted what was seen, yet was transparent. And I felt that 'I' was just such a monster eye, empty, yet *there* as well, an awkward, wobbling, ambivalent presence sited on the horrid border between liquid and solid. Sartre, when he wrote about the viscous, might have been describing my identity as I experienced it at this time:

> A slimy substance ... is an aberrant fluid ... the slimy reveals itself as essentially ambiguous because its fluidity exists in slow motion; there is a sticky thickness in its liquidity; it represents in itself a dawning triumph of the solid over the liquid ...
>
> Slime is the agony of water ...'[3]

For page after page Sartre catalogued the horror of the slimy or viscous, including its feminine characteristics.

111

its soft yieldingness, its sickly feminine sweetness, a docility beneath which lurks 'a surreptitious appropriation of the possessor by the possessed'. And before many pages this meditation led him to digress on how 'the obscenity of the feminine sex is that of everything which gapes open'. So perhaps my sense of ambiguity and amorphousness had to do with my gender. When I tried to grasp my identity it dribbled away between my fingers, yet clung stickily to the social fabric of which I was a part, or rather was noticeable when instead of trickling light, clean and witty as water it stuck with the slime and mess of social ineptitude. My identity, formless, ungraspable, was nevertheless, everywhere viscously, messily *there*. Once, in joke, I'd likened myself to a glittering, tinny, costume-jewellery dragon fly. Now, its carapace smashed, the costume-jewellery dragon fly exuded nasty slime.

*

At the end of the first year I felt blocked and stagnant. The last session of the year–the analytic year ended in the summer–took place on a hot but grey afternoon. A dull claustrophobia filled the room. I lay, ruminating aloud on the food I was eating, being overweight, the swelling, disgusted feeling this gave me, as though this were not really me, this greedy body. I ruminated on the cancer I had read about in a colour supplement, mentally seeing the detailed drawing of a cauliflower-like growth that took root all over the stomach. I felt blocked, jammed up, as if such a growth were spreading inside me and blocking me up. Because nothing seemed to change, frustration choked me. My work was stagnant. My life at home in the Islington dolls' house seemed stagnant. A year previously I had begun another romantic relationship. This relationship had at first seemed to promise a new freedom. Now it seemed to have become another kind of trap. I felt too weak to

escape it, yet I foresaw its ending with a sense of panic
I rarely permitted to break the surface.

But in a few months everything was to change.

Eight

The androgyny of the late sixties was not for the nymph-like girls, who, half naked and with billowing hair, sped alongside epicene, ringletted men. It was the men who had the dandy's frills, the long coats and trailing scarves. Groovy chicks in Biba's stripped to their tights and pulled on micro frocks. Mirrors all round the changing room reflected their heavy heads of hair, long stick-like limbs and tiny insect bodies, as they writhed and jostled for space in the shambles. Upstairs the androgyne men waited, deadpan.

Yet at the very end of the sixties I met a young woman who was the walking spirit of the androgynous. She was yards tall and thin, with a deep, aristocratic voice. Like the androgynous young men, she wore a frock coat of braided moss-green velvet, pink velvet bell bottom trousers, those heavy boots. Vanessa seemed magic–that aura of magic some persons have at points in their lives, maybe at turning points. She was magical because she approached life through a series of treats and toys that were at one and the same time sophisticated and childish–visits to the country, bottles of cloudy, home-made, scented, elderflower wine, hours spent painting watercolours two inches square, tubes of coloured plastic that could be blown into balloons, fortune-telling books, exotic titbits of food.

When I first visited her flat in West London I recognised it as one I'd visited in a former life. At the end of a cobbled alleyway you climbed a long flight of steps, crossed a roof, climbed more stairs inside to the attics of a cliff-like house, a Bayswater house like a

114

wedding cake, tier upon tier. I'd once been here with Percy to see an out-of-work theatrical designer of his acquaintance. Like all coincidences, this seemed immensely significant. That had been 1963. This was 1969. There was a whole era between my timid identity of then and my bright sophistication now.

This was the golden age of West London, bordered on the west by Ladbroke Grove, on the south by Notting Hill Gate, on the east by Queensway, fading away towards the Harrow Road in the north. It was a big druggy 'head' scene. In the peeling shells of those enormous, pompous houses a new culture spread like golden lichen, a new growth which was actually a symptom of decay. Every Saturday long-haired men and women in flapping, droopy clothes thronged the pavements of the Portobello Road, a fluctuating crowd edging past the old clothes stalls, the stalls with yams and plantains, the health food stores, the 'head' stores—the shops for hippies—which smelt of joss sticks and patchouli. From the pubs the raised voices poured out in a single roar. From the open windows the cadences of heavy rock ached across the streets. What Vanessa called hash was smoked in a thousand pads from the Elgin pub across the Squares and Gardens to where Westbourne Grove met the Porchester Hall.

Time passed differently in this new life. One of Vanessa's friends threw her watch away in order not to be dominated by the bourgeois hang-up of time. On the other hand Vanessa's flat was always full of young men and women with masses of time to pass or to kill. Vanessa and the two young women with whom she shared the flat were not real 'heads'. That is, they were not seriously into the drug culture or the hippy philosophy and lifestyle. But the hippy atmosphere seeped through the whole district, and so they lived in it too. The flat, like the boutiques, was both empty and

115

cluttered, had nothing ordinary in it like tables or chairs or beds. You sat on the floorboards, which were painted cream and strewn with mattresses and cushions. The rooms had dark brown walls and heavily fringed lampshades. Someone had stuck a few posters up, art nouveau women shaped like arabesques. Dusty, their corners curled. Vanessa used brown woodstain to varnish her windowpanes so that they looked like tortoiseshell. She hung silver paper curtains round her platform bed. This structure swayed when you moved around on it, and if you sat up too quickly you banged your head on the ceiling. We used to sit up there with her two kittens, marooned.

Her flatmates' friends from Oxford and public school hung about. A friend of Vanessa's called John did yoga in the passage and talked about science fiction as though it were fact. There was a roadie from a rock band. There was a girl who sold macrobiotic flapjack in the Portobello market. There was an old Etonian who sold paintings outside Green Park. There was an unsupported mother who used to wander, wan and plucky, from room to room, her child toddling patiently after her, while she waited for one of her boyfriends to take her out to dinner, the only meals she ever had. Gay-looking young men who weren't gay lay about on the cushions. Everyone played cards and practical jokes, told fortunes and drank coffee, and smoked, hour after hour, day after day. They all seemed to sleep with one another. Vanessa 'laid' the gay-looking young men too.

Mrs Z said to me: 'But surely you must be terribly jealous?' Her question surprised me. No–of course I wasn't jealous. It was all magic and marvellous, wasn't it? When I first met Vanessa we'd spent a weekend by the sea. At dawn we'd crept out to bathe. When we'd reached the long, flat shore, we stopped abruptly at the sight of two hares at play. They danced and sprang across the sand together with unselfconscious joy, and we waited until they had cavorted further along the bay before we ran naked into the sea, which turned mauve as it deepened towards the line of radiance that was the horizon.

Forever afterwards the relationship must live up to that moment. Yet from the beginning I suffered moods of tension, an unbearable irritation. I seethed with suppressed rage. This soap bubble dream–which now seems more distant, more dreamlike than any other of my former lives–was supposed to have given me a new identity, yet I hated myself as never before. It was less a soap bubble than a chrysalis, a period of transition. The Oxford dictionary definition of chrysalis runs: 'The state into which the larva of most insects passes before becoming an imago. In this state it is wrapped in a hard sheath.' Yes, that was it–a 'state' with no 'imago', no vision of the self.

The hippy life exerted an attraction over me because of its elements of risk, of danger, of going over the edge. Give up money, time, rules, it seemed to say. It promised altered states of consciousness, the abandonment of bourgeois manners, above all self-expression–'doing your thing'. In the peach smell of joss sticks and the earth smell of patchouli I sniffed the Baudelairean scent of romantic damnation and doom once again. Only I never found a danger to compel me. I was secretly bored by drugs, bored by adult toys, bored by science fiction. I hung in on the periphery. My hair was no longer short, but it wasn't yet long and curly. In Vanessa's flat I looked too neat, like a social worker. At work I was accused of looking like a hippy. I was neither here nor there.

Vanessa in her flat was in transition too. Having fun, being spaced out–she too fretted at the aimlessness of her life. And, like me, she never went the whole way.

She was sensitive, intelligent, beautiful, and painfully insecure. To be gay–for the time being–was acceptable at this edge of the permissive society, inhabited by a youth too cool, too liberal, or just too polite to object. But there was another side to her life where I belonged even less, and was not in fact acknowledged: her family.

She and I increasingly belonged in a third, Freudian life, to which Mrs Z alone seemed more and more to have the key. If Vanessa was sick after over-eating at one of the restaurants to which she was taken by the gay looking young men, it was my role to look after her. This childish and demanding side of her was dramatised when she caught measles. Vanessa's own mother perceived me as sinister and possessive. I resented and rejected the maternal role.

Yet, like so many mothers, I never insisted on what I wanted but turned my resentment inwards in self-dislike. I felt drab and stagnant. I felt that Vanessa was beautiful and the object of desire to all our friends, men and women. At her side I seemed a sort of ugly fairy Carabosse–and it was as if she felt the same, for she described me in a letter to a friend: 'Elizabeth is sort of small and stubby like a discarded prototype of what people might be. She has large round eyes and very thick eyelashes and a rather crooked nose, a great big mouth and bristly hair like pubic hair.'

I felt trapped in my chrysalis and longed to break out. But I lacked the energy, or even the courage to admit my resentment. I felt enraged and hurt when Vanessa said: 'But you don't really love me,' and clung to her, panic-stricken, as mothers do to their children.

One of Vanessa's young men proposed to her. I thought it was a joke, and went on a week's holiday to France. When I returned, there was a letter telling me she'd got married.

Of course it was humiliating. I lost face–the mask

slipped. But, worse than that, in one sense, I felt that she had dared where I had failed. She had broken out while I stayed trapped, she had gone over the edge, had changed her life dramatically, and even though the change was in a direction I should not have chosen, even though she escaped the hippy dream for the staid certainties of marriage rather than going for some wild new freedom, I nonetheless envied her. She'd been braver than me.

Years later my ex-lover met her in a train in the North of England with her children. They were living up there in grand country house style: 'I've found something I really like doing. I *do* like having babies.' My friend said: 'She seemed like a rather different person.' Her voice was still loud, deep and aristocratic. Otherwise she'd mysteriously altered: 'She didn't seem magical any more.'

This caused me to reflect on the whole notion of continuous identity and to wonder why we accept so readily the Freudian belief that identity does not change significantly in adult life. Our lives change, our situations, our luck–do we bring essentially the same 'character', the same 'personality' to new situations, or do external changes break up and reform our fluid 'selves' as stones and boulders divert a stream of water?

I thought, too, of Paul, who had worn a green carnation to school, and of whom I had also had magic expectations. Are these 'magic' persons whose lives seem charmed and exemplary bound to disappoint those whom they inevitably attract? I had been drawn to a quality in them I'd hoped would brush off on to me. But that can never happen. The atmosphere of a charmed life seems to be created out of something in the magic person that is unfulfilled, an inner dissatisfaction. The charm, the sense of having a 'special' quality, an alluring identity, may come from the

119

dammed up power of gifts that are not expressed and may not be recognised, the concentration of a refined consciousness, an exceptional intelligence, into the trivia of daily life. Or, in Vanessa's case, it may simply have been the glamour generated by her expectancy at a time when she was awaiting a purpose, was waiting for 'real life' to begin. Yet how enviable–they'd succeeded where I failed in creating an identity simply out of *being,* without *doing* anything at all. They generated an essence of identity as uselessly and beautifully as the hares at play on the shore.

Nine

It was 1970. It was a new decade. There was a new Tory government. There was unemployment. There was student unrest. There were claimants unions and radical social work. There were the grotesque tits, bums and lips of the underground newspapers, and there was women's liberation. There was the LSD trip and liberation through the schizophrenic experience. The years of hedonism had twisted into a feverish spiral. There seemed to be no limits. Anything could happen.

At the moment when Vanessa chose stability, for me everything was thrown into the melting pot. In August I stood on the corner of Knightsbridge while a grey sky hung overhead and a grey torrent of traffic and noise rolled and roared past and round me. Fumes choked me. I felt despair. In October I broke out of my passivity.

There were thirty or so carefully but casually dressed men and a few women in a seminar room at the London School of Economics. By another of those significant coincidences this was the very room in which the famous psychoanalyst had delivered his final lecture to me and my fellow student social workers almost a decade ago. Read and study Freud, he had said, of course you'll know the *Introductory Lectures* off by heart, read his letters to Fliess, they describe the birth of psychoanalysis . . .

He had been old. These new young men described how the world he'd represented was about to be changed, overthrown by us. If, for the first few weeks, the tone was that of a seminar, though harder and more aggressive, that all changed when news of the meetings got about—rumours spread and we helped them along by leafleting gay pubs in Earls Court. Soon the meetings took over the largest lecture theatre at LSE. Each Wednesday the banked-up seats were jammed, the crowd at the back spilled out of the doors, the careful casualness was displaced by the heads, the freaks, the androgynes. This was Gay Liberation.

In the Gay Liberation Front the hysterical peak of the hedonism of the late sixties and the moment of revolutionary fervour came together in an unrepeatable explosion. At huge meetings individuals rose to denounce the society that oppressed them. It was a spontaneous form of mass consciousness-raising. From the formality of LSE we migrated to a cellar in Covent Garden. Painted black, it was known as Middle Earth. Later still, we returned to the head scene, to a church hall in Notting Hill Gate.

With revivalist fervour, GLF clamoured into the streets, wore extravagant clothes, spray-painted psychiatric institutions (including the one where I worked) with slogans, invaded bookstores selling anti-gay books, and demonstrated Gay Pride in an endless round of public events. In the January mists GLF joined the huge marches against Edward Heath's Industrial Relations Bill, in the snows of March GLF joined the first Women's Liberation demonstration through central London, in the fine spring and summer GLF held 'Gay Days' in London Parks. Another, later memory of joining a crowd outside Pentonville Prison in the summer of 1972. Inside five London dockers were being held in a show of strength by the government to demonstrate their determination to curb the unions by the 'rule of law'. Outside, a trades union banner of red satin embroidered with gold, lifted aloft, swayed through the parted crowds to meet a second delegation with their banner of blue outside the prison gates–another symbolic demonstration of a different kind of power.

But that was in 1972, when life had already grown more sombre. In 1971 personalities flowered in a hot-house atmosphere of excitement and euphoria. I was no longer a Fairy Carabosse.

GLF transcended the 'head' and left scenes from which it sprang because it was precisely *not* cool, *not* peaceful and passive, *not* male and above all *not* normal. The whole point about GLF was its hysteria. Gay Liberation was a crazy, psychedelic sunburst, a shower of fireworks on the political horizon. There was always a sort of madness about it. It expressed the bubbling madness that had always seethed beneath the cool hedonism of the drug scene. And part of the mad euphoria was the feeling that a revolution was going on, that we were part of a cultural and political revolution. And in a peculiar way–for me–GLF fused and united the impossible and made a statement simultaneously that homosexuality was 'all right' and that it was 'damned'. At one and the same moment you could say 'gay is good' and 'yes, we are perverts'.

Gay Liberation arose in the way it did, as political rebellion expressing itself through sexual outrage and the breaking of taboos, partly because of the nihilism of the culture of the sixties. To take on a homosexual identity was to make a statement about rebellion as well as about one's sexual desires. It was Baudelaire's notion of revolt: 'Of all of politics I understand only one thing: the revolt.' And GLF was born out of an artistic climate, in the sixties, that had united sex, violence, death and madness in just such a pre-political mood of revolt.

Joe Orton, in his life even more than in his plays, had expressed that Baudelairean revolt. He wrote in his diary in 1967, a few months before his lover Kenneth murdered him:

> Kenneth, who read the *Observer*, tells me of the latest way-out group in America–complete sexual licence.

'It's the only way to smash the wretched civilization,' I said, making a mental note to hot-up *What The Butler Saw* when I came to re-write. 'It's like the Albigensian heresy in the eleventh century,' Kenneth said. Looked up the article in the *Encyclopaedia Britannica*. Most interesting. Yes. Sex is the only way to infuriate them. Much more fucking and they'll be screaming hysterics in next to no time.[4]

In his life the anarchy of anonymous sex in pissoirs resolved identities into hands, cocks and bottoms. In his surrealist plays the absurd, fussily conventional utterances of his characters, clichés of lower middle class life, were split open. They merely masked unreasoning and anarchic desires, just as the surface of life is only a makeshift device to create an illusion of coherence.

Gay Liberationists took this seriously and lived it out, and for some this involved identity passages that became catastrophic. One ex-public school journalist abandoned his job and devoted himself to Gay Liberation politics. He belonged to the GLF 'anti-psychiatry group' and once amazed us with his description of his single visit ever to a psychiatrist, who, instead of trying to find out what–if anything–was the matter with him, had told him his *own* life story. (There were many bizarre tales of psychiatric 'help'. One young man in search of comfort and support had been told by a counsellor he visited when depressed: 'There's nothing wrong with you–it's only like having green hair or seven legs.')

But it did not end there. The ex-journalist started to wear drag–women's clothes (a popular form of political activity in GLF). He then decided that clothes conforming to either male or female gender stereotypes were oppressive. He stayed in the commune in which he was then living, at first in a caftan, and then completely naked for weeks on end. For a long time he was chronically depressed and unemployed.

124

Some GLF men went through drag, the dole, drugs and anarchist politics to emerge on the other side in three-piece suits and 'straight' jobs. Most, of course, did not undergo such violent changes, remaining the socialists, reforming Fabians, heads or queens they had always been.

But the wearing of drag was a catalytic feature of GLF. Even the Maoists took to drag. Both Maoism and drag were extreme positions that seemed to me to be off the deep end, letting go of normality in a big way, sucking you into those depths that attracted and frightened me. The Maoists fearlessly supported even the worst excesses of Stalin and his rule–yes to the Nazi-Soviet pact of 1939, yes to the purges, yes to the Siberian labour camps. One might not agree with them, but what a daring feat of intellectual absolutism, what a leap into the unacceptable. After some months, though, the Maoists announced that they had become 'radical feminists'. They got into wearing women's clothes because that broke down sexual identity.

The women in GLF didn't like this. After all, we couldn't dress up as men–that would be only to take on the identity of the oppressor. It just wasn't true, we felt, that a man in a frock, a beard and make-up had fully shed his phallic power. And even if he had, weren't the radical queens just assuming the trappings of a kind of femininity that we, the women, were trying to cast off? But it *was* freaky. The hysteria, again, of a man in high heels and a dress dragged me down towards that nihilistic vortex of revolt. And there was also its tawdry theatricality–the smell of face powder, the tinsel garb, betrayed the unreality of it all. It was fantasy, or dreams, in action, nightmarish ambiguities of the unconscious invading the full light of day.

In the bright sun of summer the simmering hostilities stayed beneath the surface. We basked in the comradeship of the men who didn't like women. But as the evenings drew in, a sinister atmosphere of menace began to close round us. There were bombings, and Special Branch raids, and talk of the repression of the state went beyond mere rhetoric, feeding into real fears and tensions. The inauguration of the Festival of Light seemed like a new right-wing backlash poised against the movements of sexual liberation. At its first big meeting, at Central Hall, Westminster, in September 1971, a number of gay and women's liberation groups disrupted the proceedings. Disguised as clerics, nuns and ordinary born-again Christians they posted themselves amongst the audience and waited for the evening to begin. At first all seemed calm. Then, as the opportunity arose, they stood up, along with ordinary members of the audience, to speak out about their born-again sense of sin. It gradually became obvious that they were sending the whole thing up, going on for far too long about their sins. Some were roughly handled by ushers. This caused consternation amongst the real Christians, especially when one of the gays, disguised as a bishop, stood up and denounced the violent way in which protesters were being bundled from the hall. Someone let loose a flood of white mice. The atmosphere hotted up as a band of nuns ran to the front of the hall and danced a can-can. The meeting ended in uproar.

Shortly afterwards, a Festival of Light rally at Trafalgar Square was less successfully disrupted with stink bombs and a street theatre group. One of the actors was arrested and charged, tried but acquitted, for waving a carrot in an obscene manner. The police attacked a group of gay liberationists dressed up as choir boys. I noticed the gay liberationist who had dressed as a bishop at Central Hall still in episcopal gear in earnest conversation with two senior police officers. He was evidently trying to distract their attention from a disruption that was going on just behind them, but I wondered if his disguise had become part of his lifestyle–some bizarre new identity–and whether we should ever see him in his usual jeans and sweat shirt again.

I was disturbed and depressed by the bands of Christians, many of them very young, thronging into the Square. Between them and us was a gulf the depth of which they themselves seemed not to understand. Later in Hyde Park, they handed us religious leaflets, saying, with fixed and glassy smiles on their faces: 'Jesus loves you.' I wore a mauve tee shirt with a plastic Rupert Bear welded into its front, a symbol at the time of the liberationist 'Underground'. But if the deliberate frivolity of the opposition to the Festival of Light seemed childish, to send up the Jesus Freaks was more subversive than standard methods of disagreement would have been. It revealed more clearly their authoritarianism, while the heavy tactics of both police and Festival stewards looked ridiculous as a response to mockery.

Now that conflict between men and women within GLF had become endemic, with some men claiming they were more feminist than we were because they were less socialist, those of us who *were* socialists turned more in the direction of women's liberation. For the women in GLF who were radical feminists also–those who believed that the *primary* contradiction in society was that between men and women, and that male power was more deeply rooted than class power or capitalist exploitation–it was more logical anyway to work with other women than to 'waste their energy' on men.

A large group of us therefore went to the women's liberation conference at Skegness in October 1971. The drive through the twilight in a borrowed van with about ten women, some of whom I did not know; the arrival at a miners' holiday camp, with bright lights and the scramble for sleeping-bag space in one of the halls; the

127

setting up of our table of pamphlets and badges; the greetings from many women, friends or just familiar faces–I'd never met this atmosphere of anticipation and excitement before. The women had a distinctive look. Their long hair, long skirts and velvet trousers, crocheted shawls and patchwork knitting gave them an air almost of dowdiness that faded into a peculiarly British dusty picturesqueness–Bloomsbury, the pre-Raphaelites. I imagined that all of them were old hands at such conferences, that I was the only new girl. Yet for most of them too it must have been the first, since there had been only one previous conference.

Three conferences were taking place at the Skegness holiday camp that weekend: ourselves, the International Socialists (now the SWP), and a section of the National Union of Miners. Miners soon gathered round our stall, some with prurient comments, others out of genuine interest–how on earth could homosexuality be political? Beyond them, members of the International Socialists hovered hopefully in the expectation of ensnaring the odd Worker after he had turned away from this display of bourgeois decadence.

At that time the loosely-knit national organization of the local women's groups that formed women's liberation had been captured by a small group of Maoists, several of whom were men. The women's movement was for women only, so their presence was a provocation. They had organized the conference, which they had planned as a series of plenaries with themselves on a red-draped stage lecturing the audience on the principles of Marxism-Leninism. These were to be punctuated with work-shops, also chaired by them.

But there was a rebellion, in which the gay liberation women's group played a decisive part. One of our number took over the microphone and proposed that we should break up into small groups, according to the

128

principles of the women's movement, and discuss the topics that interested *us*; sexuality, child care, the family, lesbianism.

The rebellion gathered momentum throughout the whole of Saturday. At the disco in the evening, women danced in big, sweeping circles–celebratory. On our return to the hall where we slept we realized that our sleeping companions included the half dozen Maoists. They had taken up a position on the stage and had drawn the curtains round it to create a *cordon sanitaire* between themselves and the forces of anarchism we represented. The next morning I was woken by the sound of the curtain being drawn back. It was seven o'clock. The Maoist leader was sitting up in his sleeping bag and reading aloud from Chairman Mao's *Little Red Book*. It was almost as bad as the born-again Christians.

There was uproar at the final plenary session. The Maoists had attempted to split off the lesbians from the rest of the conference by denouncing us as part of bourgeois decadence. A member of their group, who appeared herself to be gay, had solemnly assured us over a drink at the bar that we would all–rightly–be liquidated after the Revolution. The Maoists could not however split us off because we stoutly proclaimed our socialism. Instead it was they who, after noisy hours of argument, shouting and seizing of the microphone, were led from the hall by the caretaker. Their leader gesticulated, shouting that we were flying in the face of historical truth, turned to harangue the bewildered porter and accused him of being a traitor to his own class. The event ended in exhaustion, but a sense of victory. Never had I lived so completely in the present, from moment to moment.

*

That weekend marked the high point–and also the end– of the period of my life when my lesbian identity achieved a kind of unitary coherence because it fused my

129

socialism and my sexual politics, while politics itself became a way of life. The splits, the conflicts, the confusions, the oppression tended afterwards to wear down that powerful sense of a political self. But it remained as a reference point, a centre of political conviction round which identity could ebb and flow.

It was never enough, of course, to say: 'I'm gay and I'm proud.' Satisfying as a gesture of defiance, of anger, of strength, it left too many questions unanswered. Gay liberation did, though, make me more conscious of the massive contradictions we all have to endure throughout our lives. It heightened my awareness of this not in its sober and more reasonable moments, but when it was at its maddest, at its most surreal and bizarre.

One hot, grey, summer day in 1972 I crossed London by Underground. I was carrying a basket containing two puking kittens destined for a home with a gay liberationist in the distant South London suburb of Balham. I emerged from the underground station into unknown territory. Worried and preoccupied, I wandered through the back streets of Balham in the heavy, oppressive, privet-smelling atmosphere–in the heat of summer privet smells of smouldering rubber–past primly net-curtained houses, silent in the thundery calm.

At last I found the Gothic Edwardian cottage for which I was looking. It was two o'clock in the afternoon. The sun suddenly came out. I knocked–silence. I knocked again, then a third time. At length my knocking aroused a dog inside the house. It began to bark loudly. After I had banged on the door several more times it was opened by an Apollo-like young man dressed only in bright red underpants and a gold earring. Behind him menaced one of the largest dogs I have ever seen. It appeared to be slavering to get at the kittens, who would have provided it only with a light snack.

I entered the house. The curtains were drawn and the

130

electric light created an atmosphere of unreality–as if, inside the house, we were cut off from the world. I let the kittens out in the sitting room while the dog was dragged away. After a cup of coffee and a desultory conversation I left, abandoning the kittens, I could not help feeling, to an uncertain fate. As I walked back through the suburban roads I felt that the Hansel and Gretel house with its astonishingly beautiful occupant imprisoned, it seemed, within it, cut off from the flat, uptight, surrounding streets, from the tight-lipped houses with their closed eyes and from the quiet roads where nothing ever happened and where nothing was ever meant to happen, represented the secret world of our imagination. The Apollo in the red underpants was the spirit of that secret anarchy that lurks behind the net curtains of straight society. He is the secret surrealist in us all.

Ten

For the whole of 1971, the year of my intense involvement with Gay Liberation, I continued to see Mrs Z three times a week. My sessions with her ran alongside my political activity, a fiery, larval stream of the new aggressive, political hedonism parallel with the underground trickle of the unconscious, a strange, hysterical split in my life. I never resolved the tension between my membership of GLF with its hatred of psychiatry and psychoanalysis (a hatred I at least partly shared), and my flickering sense of the purpose of psychoanalysis. It was true that the practices of psychiatry and psychotherapy tended to be sexist and anti-homosexual, to militate also against the liberation of women. It was true, too, that Mrs Z was a true liberal for whom both subjectivity and the discipline of reality were truer than politics, which–I believe like most psychoanalysts–she saw ultimately as a form of evasion, almost, you might say, of false consciousness. One day she let slip the remark: 'I don't think you have ever taken Gay Lib. too seriously,' and I interpreted this as meaning that *she* did not take it seriously, did not understand its importance, or see how sexuality could be political.

At the same time, though, Mrs Z patiently unpicked and untangled all the negative, the thwarted and twisted responses in one's life. But GLF emphasized the positive. Mrs Z believed in patience and compromise, GLF in extreme desires. To undergo these incompatible experiences simultaneously was, inevitably, to polarise them, and to increase the tension of both. Yet the tension itself made for a heightened consciousness, a feeling that at

132

one and the same time I was willing myself out of passivity, that I had broken out of the chrysalis in one great burst, and that I was slipping down into those dark unconscious depths. The foaming breakers of revolution churned against the shore. I was both tossed in their rough, exhilarating rollers and going further and further out to sea.

I have often looked back to the self of before 1970, and have said, as my ex-lover said of Vanessa: 'She's really rather a different person now.' I have often been tempted to ask whether it was GLF or Mrs Z that made it possible for me to 'break out'. But of course it was the coincidental combination of the two that created what I experienced as a new identity. Both the GLF and the Mrs Z stance to life had their own integrity, their validity. To have experienced both at once was to have more than doubled the impact of each.

*

In the third year, my therapy was broken off. It remained an incomplete and fragmentary experience. It was as if even my own experience of therapy had, somehow, to enact my ambivalence and doubts about the whole process, my on-the-threshhold attitude.

After it had ended, I continued to ruminate on it, and I still often think of Mrs Z. For a long time I found it hard to assess at all. At the end of 1972, a year after it had ended I wrote:

A Farewell to Psychoanalysis

Psychoanalysis, similar to Protestant Christianity, relies on or feeds off introspection. An intellectual process to release feeling. Is this possible, even?

There is the obvious–trite–contrast between the psychoanalyst's interpretation of the relationship as a process of liberation, and my own experience of it as constrained or constraining; normative.

133

The emphasis was on compromise–the compromise between the limitations of reality and the unbounded desires of the psyche–a bourgeois notion of cutting your coat according to your cloth. Of course it is common sense that one cannot transcend one's limitations. And yet the unbounded desires are themselves a kind of reality.

I was offered the experience of 'being understood'. And it is true that as a result my past now stands in a different perspective. I am more in touch with the guilt produced by my childhood.

The good-little-girl image is dissipated ... that goes back to one's self image.

What I understand now is the child I was then.

At the bottom of it all was a curious mixture of normative views and subjectivism (what you *really* want is your *real* happiness and at some level you have a right to it). I certainly allowed this to affect me in that I'm more jealous of my rights these days–but sometimes I just come out as an angrier person. I feel I'm more outgoing, open, and overtly aggressive.

In order wholly to transcend masochism one has also to be able to release one's vitality and I don't know to what extent I've been able to do this.

I always liked my analyst and thought of her as not censorious.

This now seems a rather grudging response to an impressive person who I believe did understand me. On two occasions in 1974 I went to see Mrs Z to talk about a difficult, unhappy love affair. Only then did I fully appreciate her gift–and her skill–of 'understanding'. Sometimes when I'd been in continuous therapy with her, her remarks had seemed banal or alienatingly 'liberal'. But to enter her consulting room in 1974 was to step back into that atmosphere of 'understanding' as if my last visit had been the previous day. I'm not sure why her recognition of 'how I feel', of my *self*, was so comforting. It spoke to an identity, perhaps, different from those masks, those moods, those jagged-edged shards of mirror that represented my multiplicity of selves. This sense of being understood was not a self, not an identity, but was more like a space where hard edges of identity did not have to be so sharply etched out, where oneself, simply as an interplay of feelings, could float, suspended securely in this ethos of understanding. What I am describing is, I suppose, something like a womb.

*

I had thought when I became involved in gay liberation, and later in the women's movement, that I had in all essentials left psychoanalysis behind. Far from it. My life was haunted in the seventies, as the women's movement itself was haunted, by the Freudian path into the hinterland of the unconscious, which, if we feminists trod it, might lead to the source and origins of women's subordination.

In November 1974 I wrote:

> Friday evening–the beautiful house, a rose red room filled with baubles and knick knacks. A giant typewriter under its cover. A delicate, reserved élite dissecting the work of Lacan, savouring some poetic quality in his abstruse symbolism. In unravelling the obscurities of Lacan they seemed to make enormous assumptions about Freud; if anything was referred back to Freud it was with no breath of criticism or doubt. His was the ultimate authority. The only time I tried to raise this and talk about the problems in his theory, I was made to feel vulgar and intrusive. So whereas I should have liked to discuss my *confusions* about Freud, they operated on a certainty.

This was my description of my single visit to a psychoanalytic study group, a visit that reawakened or reinforced my doubts. I couldn't assimilate my emotional experience to their intellectual conviction. It was simply a baffling, alienating gap.

All the same—psychoanalysis was the mirror of the age. One always returned to Freud, for after all, he had invented a therapeutic method which explored the *narrative* that a life might be—identity as autobiography. He had invented that curious verbal mirror, the psychoanalytic hour, in which the self is explored via the medium of an Other in recognition that identity is not a discrete self, but a relationship and a process.

And, for Freud at least, the psychoanalytic experience was not just a conformative process, but was about personal liberation from the prison of narcissism. The Freudian journey back through time was not to reinhabit the narcissistic self of infancy gazing in the mirror pool at its own reflection, but was to loosen one's anchorage in the past.

Freud also provided the only theory of sexual development as social process. That was attractive to feminists, who wanted to discuss and to understand the strange contradictions of sexual feeling, but had and have enormous difficulty in so doing.

Time and again at women's conferences on sexuality (where, as my former lover remarked, it seems possible to discuss sexuality only in large groups of a hundred or more) there was a sense of bafflement and struggle. Part of that struggle is with the heritage of the sixties. The 'new politics', after all, was born in the sixties when radicals were influenced by the tainted, sub-Freudian baggage of western culture, of which an obsession with identity and selfhood is so much a part. From the beginning this new politics was personalised to the limits, so that even madness became a form of conscious protest, while sexuality was seen as the overturning of repression. To make love was to break out of the character armour of the bourgeois self.

But while there was a sense in which the feminist return to Freud was a healthy reaction against Wilhelm Reich's dream of the revolutionary orgasm, it never engaged with the search of those women who, still influenced by the broken promises of the sixties for an unfettered sexuality, continued to hope for revolutionary love. Could we ever be an army of lovers? To this the Freudian feminists had no answer. They withdrew, either to marvel at the cultural construction of femininity, or even to reaffirm Freudian traditionalism. The complexity of the Freudian interpretation, its intricacy and attention to detail, made the slogans and campaigns of the activists seem intolerably naive and crude.

The struggle to construct a 'liberated' sexuality, the continuing influence of 'radical therapy' and the return to Freud coexisted throughout the seventies within the women's movement. In 1974 there was a sexuality conference about which I wrote afterwards:

> January 13th—yesterday the women's conference on sexuality. It was all very confused and earnest—a hundred women in a smoke-filled hall at North London Polytechnic, all dressed in the picturesquely dowdy manner of the movement—struggling and yearning towards some resolution of their unhappiness and disappointment. I felt sad afterwards, that there was really something sad about the communal aspiration towards a fuller and more fully expressed emotional life, one in which we were not so held back and hampered by our frustration and the tangles of our feelings. One woman spoke of the contradiction between wanting to be 'strong women' and spontaneous sexual fantasies of surrender and masochism. There was an argument because some women claimed that lesbian relationships were without jealousy and

137

pain (I just felt they were saying that they don't fall in love with women the way they do with men).

There was another, socialist feminist, day conference on sexuality in London in 1977. The groups this time were smaller, but found discussion no easier. The group I was in split between those who supported and those who were critical of all forms of psychotherapy. For one woman, herself a 'radical therapist', therapy was a way on from consciousness raising, a form of liberation. For another it was a repressive practice, which had caused her to suspend her (lesbian) sexual life for more than a decade.

Then there was the other side to it all. One wintry day at the end of 1978 I visited a feminist with whom I'd once worked politically in the women's movement. These days we seldom met. She gave me lunch. She was absorbed in child care. I liked her children, but it was as if she felt she had to be apologetic, or felt that I could never understand the pull of motherhood. The real problem, she said suddenly, was not careers, which were really a form of penis envy. The real problem was that we had failed as feminists to value women's work. Nothing was amiss with a domestic role for women, only that we had not given it sufficient status.

I hurried away down the street and found myself in a cold, pale, stucco square. I sat down and burst into tears of rage. She had used Freud to justify her views, and I felt betrayed, by the fickleness of the political climate, by wilfully changing fashions in ideas, and by what seemed to me a facile adoption of ideas with which I'd struggled and of a theory I'd experienced as sometimes affirmative but often restricting over years of frustration and pain. As Winifred Holtby put it: '"Good wives and mothers" shut themselves up in the comfort of their private lives and earn the approval of unthinking society.'[5]

It was not that I did not agree with my friend's

138

estimation of 'women's work'. The difference was, it seemed to me, that I did not believe it should be reserved for women, but believed that it was as important for men to share in the 'caring role' as it was for women to work out in the world.

I sobbed stupidly in the empty square, disconcerted by the strength of dominant ideals, disconcerted not just by one trivial incident, but by a general failure of nerve, by our continuing need for approval. Our beliefs falter–we cease to believe that anything can change. We blame ourselves for having dared to aspire to a place alongside men in the big, wide world.

I was angry too because of the defensiveness and the reproachfulness of even feminist mothers. Why had I no children? Simply because as a gay woman in the sixties it had never seemed to be an option. Women did not in those days choose, on the whole, to have babies outside marriage, certainly not middle class women like me. We had known one lesbian couple who managed, against all the odds, to adopt a child. They had had to fight a ferocious battle with the child care officers over it.

Too many feminists, though, assumed that childless-ness was rationally chosen, gave one, unasked and unwanted, the cold identity of non-mother by choice, turned one into a strong woman, an iron maiden with no softness, no uncertainty, and, ultimately, no feelings. In this way reactionary ideologies return amongst the very groups that fought them most strongly.

Moreover, feminists have made a kind of self-identifica-tion with their feelings. At first the source of their oppression was located in the outside world. Then the interest shifted to the internalisation of that oppression in one's psyche. At a third stage, the explanation (often Freudian) of these 'reactionary' feelings (longings for passivity, masochism, the martyrised exaggeration of a longing to serve) somehow begins to justify them. Real women *do* feel like that, and so perhaps they should, goes the implied argument. It seems more gutsy, somehow. We don't want to be cold and rationalistic like men, after all, so we begin to sink back into the stereotyped identities of womanhood that society has held up for us to imitate all along.

*

My experience of psychoanalytic therapy never resolved my ambivalence towards Freudian theory. My relationship with Mrs Z was a rewarding one, despite its limitations, and it convinced me of the validity of the therapeutic method of free association–of just saying whatever came into your head. Mrs Z was very good at unpicking the trivial events in daily life that triggered off my anger, despair and guilt, and in relating them back to childhood distress she left me in no doubt that the unresolved problems of our early years do in some way continue to dog us in adult life. The theories Freud developed to explain the material elicited by his method still seem less satisfactory, although he was surely right to see both heterosexuality and 'masculinity' and 'feminity' as social creations, end products of a process, and fragile at that.

In the spring of 1979 I had a dream, which I wrote down because it seemed significant. I had been to see an Ingmar Bergman film, *Autumn Sonata*. The film investigates the relationship between a brilliantly successful concert pianist and her unhappy, self-punishing daughter. The mother cannot accept emotion, nor care for either of her daughters (her other daughter is paralysed) while the daughter can find neither release from her raging emotions, nor self fulfilment. The film uncovers the hatred and rage seething beneath her apparent love for the mother for whose rare visit she so eagerly waits and prepares.

The audience in the cinema where we saw the film was a disturbed one. Two women refused to sit where directed and began an angry scene during the main film, objecting loudly to its cruelty and the painful scenes with the paralysed daughter. Others in the audience seemed to object equally to the quarrelling pair–themselves a mother and daughter, it appeared–and to the relationships depicted on the screen. There were ripples of unease. A woman along the row from me burst into tears. Another hid her head in her hands.

That night I had a dream. I used to have a recurring dream, which is always different in detail but is always essentially the same. I am living in an untidy house and it is of great concern to me. At its worst it is a nightmare. Often it is slightly creepy and sinister. Sometimes the house is being cleared out and freshly painted. The architectural details of the house are usually vivid and never the same. Yet it always *is* the same house.

The next day I wrote:

> I had a dream in which I was going to see Mrs Z again. She was living with another woman and their house was very untidy–it was like the dream I so often have about my own house–the whole place falling apart, untidy and rather dirty rooms–little strange side rooms etc. I went up several flights of stairs and found her eventually–and it became clear to me that she was the concert pianist mother of the film–who's portrayed as having failed her daughter–she kicked the (analytic) couch out from under her huge grand piano and we faced each other. There was a feeling of social embarrassment and neither of us knew what to say–I clasped my hands together, and then finally sat down and managed to say: 'I've come to see you because I'm uneasy about my femininity.'

Eleven

Femininity was an intangible, unreal essence of self that could never be realised, but masculinity was equally nebulous. These misty qualities attaching to gender veiled the variety of actual individuals. Femininity, really, had been for me simply the theme of a lecture society had been giving me—at home ('be a little lady'), at school, in women's magazines, through the mouthpiece of boy-friends—ever since I could remember, almost. And its message was that the jack-in-the-box self that was always breaking through the chrysalis of 'manners' and 'good behaviour' was unacceptable. That bottled-up self, the most authentic self I recognised, was not particularly a gendered self at all. Moments of spontaneity seemed to transcend the sterile poses required by masculinity and femininity. These couldn't account for—say—the volup-tuous passivity of a (heterosexual) male friend, or for the virility of a woman I knew, a virility brought out in her not by lesbianism but by motherhood.

To experience one's body as physical, as corporeal, was also less closely related to a sense of gender than might have been expected. Sexual love, for example, so often described (for women at least) in terms of loss of self and abandonment, was actually the source of a heightened sense of self for me, and I discovered with the advent of the women's movement that other women felt the same. For example:

> When Anna was born ... I laughed the same laugh that I have since sometimes laughed after orgasm. It is not a pretty laugh, it frightens Anna ('Don't make love. Please don't make that noise, I can't stand it')

142

and also my lover. It is a laugh of power, the strength of life flowing throughout my body.[6]

I did not experience this sense of potency in terms of masculine or feminine at all, simply as a sense of self. And there is certainly no simple relationship between masculine and feminine and heterosexual or homosexual eroticism. Some women have described how in love-making with men they felt masculine, and it was only with women that their femininity flowered, while homosexual love between men may be a celebration of maleness, as the leather and muscle bars of the gay subculture suggest. Other women do undoubtedly assert a sense of masculinity in their lesbian relationships. The style developed, for example, in lesbian literary circles between the wars, seems to have revolved around a dandified masculine pose, as the paintings of Romaine Brooks illustrate.

But underneath–Truman Capote described a visit he paid to Romaine Brooks's deserted studio with her lover Natalie Clifford Barney in 1948:

> There they were: Lady Una Troubridge with a monocle in her eye; Radclyffe Hall in a marvellous hunting outfit with a terrific hunting hat. It was the all-time ultimate gallery of all the famous dykes ... and of course Miss Barney herself in a wonderful outfit with a pair of gloves here and a whip in the foreground ... that's what made the whole thing so eerie ...
>
> It had so little to do with the Miss Barney I was standing with, this cosy little Agatha Christie-Miss Marple lady ... this chirpy pigeonlike little lady who had so little relationship to this ... wild thing wearing a cravat, with her hand on her hip like *this,* and a *whip* over there ... this dominating woman with a whip.[7]

143

*

Lesbianism, I think, was meant to give me a transcendent identity that would melt masculinity and femininity together in some new and potent sense of self that improved upon both. But what was a lesbian identity? Lesbians too were confused about lesbian identity and lesbian sexuality. And I certainly wanted no-one to think of me as a Radclyffe Hall, or to say of me, 'What a pity she's not a man.'

In the mid sixties my lover and I met some other lesbians in London and in the Midlands, through a contact group that was set up at that time. We met women whose lives were locked in secrecy, women for whom the accident of falling in love with another woman had had strange and imponderable social ramifications, women for whom the question of identity was an unresolved and pressing problem.

Once, my lover was invited as speaker to a local group. We drove out to the village in the green hills where the meeting was to take place, and found the right house, a neat, modern bungalow with crazy paving and bulging windows. Fifteen or so women waited for us in the comfortable living room. The atmosphere of the room, though, was not one of comfort. I myself felt a tension. It was a warm evening, but a fire had been lit in the rustic grate, and I was positioned next to this, seated on a leather 'pouffe'. A huge, alarming Alsatian lay at my other side.

My friend began her talk. Her subject was the development of homosexuality as a social role. But it soon became clear that this was not quite what had been expected. Before long a voice cried: 'What d'you expect, though–I mean, if I'm in bed with my girl friend, I don't expect to *do* anything–I mean she's butch, I tell her she's the one to do all that. I'm not interested in history, the point is, should I be expected to *do* anything or not?'

144

A stricken silence; both hostess and speaker smoothed the matter over as best they could, but the audience was restless and the questioner retired in tears to another room. Afterwards there was a discussion in which we tried to come to grips with the thorny issue of masculine and feminine identities, of 'butch' and 'femme'.

Several years later, in Gay Liberation, it struck me that for male homosexuals the question of roles, although not unimportant, did not have this compulsive interest; for men the questions of 'cottaging' (picking up sexual partners in lavatories) and 'cruising' (picking up generally) seemed more urgent. The expression of their sexuality was what interested them. Lesbians (in the sixties at any rate) had hardly known what their sexuality *was*. Although it would be misleading to make too much of the problem of 'butch' and 'femme' roles, the very fact that they existed, and that some women had, in particular, a strong attachment to the playing of a male role, signified *something*. Our hostess on the occasion of the talk, herself rather boyish, declared with massive tolerance that she didn't care if her girlfriend lay on a sofa all day and ate chocolates so long as they were both happy, but it was not just a question, as we all dimly realised, of who held the door open and who went through it first. Nor was it a question simply of 'being happy'. What then *did* it mean? Why did Danny, whom I'd known in the early sixties, think of herself as 'him'?

Many lesbians rejected the idea of being paired off as masculine and feminine, but how else *could* we be defined? This ignorance and confusion expressed real suffering, real longing. In all of us, I suppose, lurked an unacknowledged ambivalence not so much towards men as towards masculinity. On the one hand, rejecting men, why should we wish to ape them? On the other hand, for some women the right to play an active role in a man's world—in the world of work—seemed to bring with it the

145

playing of a more general social role of male. Did this social potency, then, bring with it some sort of sexual potency? Did we equate lesbianism with potency? Or was lesbianism a rejection of femininity? After all, femininity was unsatisfactory as an expression of independence. Yet if we rejected femininity, how could we desire women?

We stumbled about, confused by a debate that was cast within not one but several wrong frameworks. Were we, for example, trying to find out what we 'really' were, masculine or feminine, and what would make us 'really' happy–seeking some core or bedrock of an essential lesbian self? This essentialism was one framework (never spelt out). Another was simple moralism. This emphasised the wrongness of exaggerated social roles, and disapproved especially of women who were male in an extreme way. Rejection of overdone role-playing was part of gay Fabianism, part of the effort to assert our normality. And although Simone de Beauvoir had hinted at the mysterious contradiction of lesbianism when, in *The Second Sex* she had written: 'They live like men in a world without men', she hadn't explained this dilemma or pointed any way out of it.

Perhaps we sought an androgyny that would have wiped out these problems. The ambiguity and light-heartedness of androgyny was, however, conspicuously absent from the whole heavy debate about roles.

A few years later, when I was on my round of visits to psychoanalysts, one of the 'permissive' ones asked me to name my ideal sexual object. Having just seen Bunuel's film *Belle de Jour* I suggested the androgynous hero. We discussed whether the point was that he was effeminate (like a woman) or that he was in spite of this actually a man. He, I later decided, expressed *active* androgyny, an erotic ambiguity that was effeminate yet active, whereas the androgyny of women is usually ultimately passive. The beauty of Garbo or Dietrich, however tantalizingly male, is always in the end returned to submission or vacancy. Garbo is most typically Garbo in the famous last shot of *Queen Christina* when she gazes, without blinking, endlessly out to sea, impassive. She is less 'herself' in the earlier scenes, stomping around in boots like a principal boy. And then, although Dietrich often appears in drag in her films, she too is always returned to femininity. In *Morocco,* as a small-time nightclub singer she performs in to hat and tails, and, during her song, she tosses a carnation towards the legionnaire she fancies. In men's clothes she is actively sexual and provocative, yet the final shot of the film tracks her as she limps submissively out into the desert, meekly, hopelessly following her man.

(There was a sequel to this conversation about the Bunuel hero when, several years later, I had a brief affair with a similar androgynous young man. I discovered that his temperament was closer to the passivity of a Garbo than to the frenetic activity of the Bunuel hero–a case of life not matching fantasy.)

When, in the sixties, I'd mediated my sense of inferiority by declaring myself an aesthete or a hedonist, rather than being feminine I'd been effeminate, a dandy. My preoccupation with style and sensation declined into a kind of camp stance to life. And I think now that this attempt at androgyny lay on a knife edge of romanticism. Camp, for all its malice, its cynicism, its cool parody, plays with the notion of the impossible narcissistic love for oneself, for one's twin, for one's alter ego, and, like romanticism, it elevates the impossible to the pinnacle of highest desire. It flirts, too, equally with sexual perversity and with sexlessness, and is in many ways a cerebral sexual style.

Wasn't this kind of romanticism present, too, in my attraction to Vanessa, another longed-for self, perhaps, who failed (necessarily) to give me an androgynous identity? And even in Gay Liberation, wasn't it there too, in a kind of male identification with those beautiful young men?

Homosexuality itself, moreover, was for many years one facet of my general romanticism about life. Romanticism could be vividly embodied in tragic homosexual love.

1967–I was still in love, off and on, with Hazel. A fine summer's morning–I'd spent the night with her. We were unhappy. I walked home from the tube station, taking a different route from my usual one. In one of the quiet, gentrified, residential streets a crowd had gathered at an open door. There was an ambulance, and a sense of urgency as policemen hurried in and out. For a moment I joined the salaciously disapproving crowd, but it was only later, after listening to the news on the radio, that I realised that the house with the open door had been the scene of Joe Orton's murder by his lover, who'd then killed himself. I telephoned Hazel. I was in tears, maudlin. She seemed angry: 'that's what love's all about.'

That evening she came to see me: a wonderful, light, summer evening. I wore a long mauve dress. I played a record:

> I read the news today, oh boy,
> About a lucky man who made the grade
> And though the news was rather sad
> Well I just had to laugh
> I saw the photograph
> He blew his mind out in a car
> He didn't notice that the lights had changed.
> A crowd of people stood and stared
> They'd seen his face before . . .

We danced dreamily to the throbbing, echo-chamber chords and the pseudo-innocence of the choirboy voice. We danced in the small front room, easily seen from the

148

street, like two mechanical dolls, turning in a lighted box in a clockwork representation of true love.

Twelve

The mystery of identity has many ways in. One image I have is of a piece of coral or a sponge, organic matter with a shape and with multiple entrances that are also exits. Perhaps identity would be especially like a sponge, which soaks up substances and becomes heavy and moist, while it can also be dry and light. Walter Benjamin described the past–which is part of one's identity–as a maze, but the image of a maze suggests that there exists a right path to the heart of the maze, to the core of self, when perhaps no such core is to be found. What *is* identity then? Is it a face in the mirror? The idea of reflection seems far too simple. Gertrude Stein implied that the self is simply an opaque surface, and in her book *The Autobiography of Alice B Toklas* (which is an autobiography of herself) she tends to reject the idea of an ongoing continuity of identity. She is rather the self painted by Picasso, whose portrait of herself she describes–a self seen from outside, not an inner self of feeling states, of emotions and thoughts.

Perhaps identity is the home-movie of memory that flickers forever in the darkened room of the mind, like a TV set left on even when no one is watching. But you never see the same movie twice—and the reels in your head are certainly changing all the time.

Is identity then a stylized mask, personality as display, as disguise, as role? The theatrical metaphor does gesture towards an ambiguity between reality and fiction when it comes to the way in which the problem of identity fascinates many people.

Some sociologists have suggested that the modern obsession with 'identity' arises out of the split that has occurred between public and private life. Private life becomes the zone of security and stability, where the essential core of self resides, while public life is both the zone of transformation, change and progress, and also the sphere in which our identities are reduced to a bureaucratized statistic. Your identity dwindles to a number— your clocking-in number, your bank account number, your social security number. You are stopped at frontiers and in entrance halls and asked for 'proof of identity'. To flash the little card or booklet with its photograph is to be accepted as both innocent and verifiable. Yet in itself, this compulsory act produces a reaction of rebellion or even of guilt, if not of guilty triumph—they don't know who I really am, what I really think. Those lines of travellers departing, returning, always look furtive and uneasy. There are so many secrets, so many selves that jar with the official version: 'I smuggle dope'—'I've done time'—'I organized the kidnapping'—'I'm travelling with my mistress'—'my father raped me'—disreputable or at least inadmissible selves throng invisibly around us.

This negative idea of one's true identity as a guilty secret is but one version of the metaphor of identity as mask, and of an essential identity hidden behind the screen of appearances. The implication of the search for a 'true' identity is that the true self is the hidden, private self. When I was eleven and reading Baroness Orczy, and equally when I was eighteen and reading Proust, I thrilled romantically to Sir Percy Blakeney because he was *really* the Scarlet Pimpernel, and to Odette de Crécy because she was *really* a lesbian and a whore (or was she?).

The sociologists who emphasised the split between public and private saw the public sphere in terms of mobility and change, and from that point of view autobiography became a migration through successive selves, and the metaphor of life was a journey, a picaresque adventure. One had no ongoing self. The

151

changing social sphere called forth new personas. The exciting part of the exploration of the private was the hope of finding the 'real' self; the excitement of seeing one's life as a journey was to find new selves.

Neither metaphor quite reflects the ambiguity of identity. For identity is neither public mask nor private heart of hearts, nor is it just a narrative. Rather it is the threshhold between private interiors—worlds of fantasy—and the public domain where we become performers. It is a private part of ourselves that we nonetheless display, hence its ambiguity. The word 'identity' is no more than shorthand for a jumble of contradictory performances, anxieties and desires. The performance is a confused one because it is not just consciously willed. The unconscious acts upon it. It has to be seen as the interface of consciousness and unconsciousness. It is changing and yet the same, like light shimmering on water.

*

I did not enter the women's movement in search of an identity. Political activity simply presented itself to me as an imperative and as an escape, a liberation from the privatised obsessions of the search for identity.

The radical movements of the late sixties and of the seventies did, though, raise the question of personal identity in a way no political movement had raised it before. Earlier socialists may have tried to raise questions of the personal life, but only now was a culture already saturated with the individualism of popularised psychotherapies awaiting the revolution of everyday life. Changed consciousness had become a necessary part of revolutionary change.

Yet this heightened and fractured sense of individual identity—a key feature of modern Western culture—which charged the radical movements with power, has also acted as a brake upon them. For it has become ever more chancy for revolutionaries to rely on the once powerful appeal of solidarity with a class or group. We failed to develop a collective subjectivity.

Feminists found this too. At first it seemed enough for women to speak out. If they did this, they would find themselves, and find themselves together. Many of the journals and books of the movement have names that suggest this, for instance *Women's Voice–Another Voice–Call to Women*, and if there is a typical literary form of feminism it is the fragmented, intimate form of confessional, personal testimony, autobiography, the diary, 'telling it like it was'.

The idea that women need only throw off their oppression for a 'real' self to appear is, nonetheless, oversimplified. Can we really say that our socially constructed 'feminine' identity is merely a husk to be discarded as we bite into the kernel, or a chrysalis the butterfly breaks out of? Women have spoken out, have given testimony as if the 'truth' of their experiences were transparent and straightforward. But–is it?

Feminists have turned to testimonies written by women who were not or could not be part of any movement. In many such testimonies a woman's identity is built, initially at least, out of pain and suffering, out of false experience. We thrill, as if someone had drawn the edge of a razor across our flesh, to the way in which Jean Rhys tears off a layer of skin to reveal her raw experience as victim of male cruelty and indifference. We sink towards madness with Doris Lessing at the pain of that same cruelty turned on women who dare to be 'free'. Kate Millett tells of the same pain, which she hoped to escape in the women's movement, but which returned to torment her from within feminism itself.

Some women speak of the moment of optimism when at last they have thrown off the role of victim and martyr. Some go further still in finding a new identity in the women's movement.

Yet women are offered only a collective identity 'in the movement'. A new identity is assumed but remains amorphously within 'sisterhood'. The 'movement' is a vague, formless conception of the celebration of women-ness, an essence of womanhood; sometimes it is described as an endless dance in which women-loving-women sing as they circle in the weaving hand-in-hand of an embrace of all by all in which all individuality, all difference–all identity–is dissolved. Anja Meulenbelt writes of this moment:

> I dance in the crowd to the witch music ... Or just look, at women whom I have begun to find so beautiful, who dance close together in couples, who dance in groups, with swinging hair and shining eyes, proud of what they are. Grown-up and now stronger than those people who had no need to fight oppression. I am in love, I think, with a species ... I dance with old friends and new ones, my body supple ... I feel beautiful among women, am beautiful ... It is as if I have come home ... Back in mother's arms ... [8]

Thus have women tried to construct a collective identity out of a shared experience of collective oppression. For many women, the moment of commitment to the women's movement must also have seemed like the birth of a new *individual* identity: 'I am a feminist.' Yet an emphasis on the moment of collective identification, although necessary, is not enough. It can become static. It does not develop the idea of identity as process, and it also in a curious way is blind to what each of us *as an individual* brings with us into the movement. For all its emphasis on the truth of experience, it ignores–although perhaps necessarily in seeking a basis for solidarity and sisterhood–our sense of individuality and of an unique past, an unique self.

Yet we carry this unique identity forward with us in the

154

movement, after the moment of collective identification. What comes after the moment when we say: 'I am a feminist'? How do we develop a collective subjectivity that allows for difference and diversity?

Feminists have written an enormous amount about stereotypic constructions of 'feminity'. There has also been a popular stereotypic construction of 'feminist' (dungarees–no make-up–hates men–angry). But what do those feminists do who reject equally both these images from the dominant culture? Perhaps, instead of dwelling so obsessively on how femininity gets inside our heads, feminists should have thought more about how to construct a plurality of positive images of women. As it is, women have fallen back on to the notion of the 'strong woman'. But however good it is to be strong, we feel ambivalent about the strong, powerful woman, since this too is an image that allows for no moment of weakness, and cannot reflect the diversity and complexity of our desires. Women who have sought to identify with 'strong women' in the movement have sometimes been so disappointed when these turned out not to be super-human after all that they have even turned against feminism itself.

This is a form of romanticism. The contemporary radical sexual liberation movements were supposed to be grounded in a rejection of romanticism. Yet the rejection of romanticism at the individual level, at the level of personalised romantic love, was over-emphasised at the expense of any real examination of political romanticism–the longing for utopias and reconstructed selves, and the longing for the pure, revolutionary moment. That political romanticism can easily give way to a 'left wing melancholy' which stresses the inescapable awfulness of the 'society of the spectacle', our destiny as victims, the impossibility of escape.

Even more dangerously, in hard times we seek out

155

'my identity' not in the clamour of revolutionary affirmation on the streets, but in the cover of small, enclosed
spaces. We seek it, if we are lucky, in the haunts of the new
hedonism, in the hushed hour of the analytic couch, in
the jacuzzi baths, in the cult of the body beautiful, in the
discoes and restaurants of the glittering metropolis-
Manhattan heaven. If we are less privileged we may seek
it in the harsh consolation of cult churches or even in the
rhetoric of fascism with its deliberate, seductive elevation
of the irrational, its call to the unconscious. Socialist and
revolutionary movements seem somehow to have lost
their ability to give the individual an enhanced identity
within the powerful safety of the movement. They have
come to be seen, all too often, as a submission to
conformity, which is the opposite of what they were
intended to be.

Feminists and radicals need some powerful sense of
identity as both collective and individualised. There is
not one tyrannical identity to which all must approximate,
but a group insistence on the value of difference. The
testimony of consciousness raising, and of those 'women's'
literary forms of diary, autobiography and confession, do
not suggest an identical experience of the world, although
the testimony has made possible the identification of
points of similarity which have formed the basis for
collective politics.

*

There is no simple reflection of oppression. We think of
writing as putting a mirror to the world, and imagine that
our readers will see in the mirror what we see. But the
mirror is more like a prism. The image changes shape
and flashes off in all directions in its collision with the
reader's consciousness. The reader always sees something of herself in our mirror.

Was the search for 'my identity' also a romanticism,
an impossibility? Personal identity may be no more

than a mirage, simply the longing to crack the mirror in order to find out what lies behind it. Ultimately the quality, flavour and nature of 'my identity' must remain a mystery, either because it is too various or because it is simply not there.

Yet even if identity is like one of those sets of Russian dolls, where to open one is to find another inside with at the heart of the smallest—emptiness, we continue to search. Even if 'my identity' is a discourse of fragments and self-contradiction, I have a subjective sense of coherence and continuity, equally though of distance and of difference (was that really me?). That is the strangeness of identity, that we experience ourselves as both fragmentary *and* coherent.

Identity is like Alice's looking-glass house and looking-glass world, a world in which you have to walk in the opposite direction in order to reach your destination, a world in which Alice's implied question remains un-answered:

> Let's consider who it was that dreamed it all . . . You see . . . it *must* have been either me or the Red King. He was part of my dream, of course—but then I was part of his dream, too!

*

In the autumn of 1978 I visited, with a friend, an exhibition of women's art. It was the second of three Indian summers in London, October days gilded and blue, hot, hard, enamel days. But in the early morning the sun lacked heat and the air was fuzzy with mist.

We crossed Waterloo Bridge to the South Bank, passed the gloomy region beneath the concert halls where the shrieks of children echoed as they swooped on skateboards round the concrete saucer between the squat supporting columns, and ascended a spiral staircase to the art gallery. Once inside, we joined other spectators in wandering from room to room. There were not so many as to make a crowd.

157

I watched the others, and thought what a strange thing it was to walk round public rooms looking at objects on the walls, objects whose purpose, amongst other things, was that they lacked all useful purpose, even in a sense the purpose of decoration, since, as 'works of art' they claimed to be more than decorative.

I sat for a while, and watched the spectators looking at the works of art. All, without having consciously learnt it, had a special way of walking round the exhibition. They held their noses a little in the air, and paused in a profound way before each work of art, bored, judicious and absorbed all at the same time. They did not pause too long, nor hurry on. They had, in fact, perfected a refined form of loitering. I decided that perhaps the real pleasure in looking at works of art was that it gave you *carte blanche*, as an adult, to loiter, as children will pause and stare when they become absorbed in some trivial object in the street. Adults may not loiter in the streets, and so they have built these special places–art galleries–in which loitering is the accepted mode of progression.

The works of art were mostly not paintings. The artists seemed rather to have been trying to reconstruct atmospheres or enterprises, although there was a huge, realistic bronze horse on the terrace, a piece of sculpture my friend especially liked. There was a series of colour photographs of a burning high-heeled shoe. There was a room devoted to the recreation of the process of excavation of an ancient Greek site. There was a corner of the exhibition that had become part of a reconstituted room, thirties style. I stood in it for a few moments, interested in this discarded shell of some personality which was only to be vaguely apprehended by standing in the 'room', yet which was palpably there. Then there was an exhibit entitled 'The Last Supper'. This was a table around which chairs were arranged. Above these, plaster joints of meat of various kinds hung from butcher's hooks. You watched them to

158

the accompaniment of soupy, swooping choral music as they moved slowly, swaying a little, round the chrome rail from which they were suspended. Nearby was another exhibit, a model of a body on a mortuary slab. When you sat down to look at it, as the positioning of a chair invited you to do, you saw on the TV screen which formed the head, or in which the head of the body should have rested, your own face videoed onto the screen.

At last we came to the most discussed exhibit, a whole room in which was charted the progress of the artist's baby through infancy. The baby's first nappies were framed on the wall, little cotton scraps, palely stained. I was reminded of those scraps of material preserved in museums of ancient civilizations. The baby's first scribbles and its first babblings were likewise preserved from oblivion, the linguistic process charted by means of a printing set, the letters set in a frame. Over the infant's first messy scrawls on coarse, grey recycled paper the mother had written a diary, neat comments on her feelings and responses to his progress. The infant became a child. Now there were artefacts reconstructed to look like exhibits in a natural history museum, which enshrined a stone, a stick, a leaf, found by the child and given to his mother (the refuse, as Freud said, of the phenomenal world). The exhibit was, in fact, a Freudian account of how a human baby, a primarily biological entity, becomes a subjectivity, how identity grows from exploration of the world, and also through relationship with the mother–so identity is, in part, the process of relationship after all.

There we encountered a woman we'd known long ago in revolutionary circles, Rosa. She was still larger than life, was still the girl a famous film director had wanted to star in his revolutionary movies. He had seen her during a university sit-in, which he was filming–there were cars set on fire, riots on the campus, nude love-ins–and had walked straight up to her and asked her to be in his film.

Instead, Rosa had later, and after much more serious events, gone to prison. And now that great slab of cold turkey, the prison years, lay between us. Yet Rosa looked as much *too much,* so much larger than life, as ever. The three of us wandered into another room of the exhibition. One of the constructs in this room was a room within a room, with floor and ceiling of mirrors. When you looked down between your feet you saw the dizzying reflection of infinity as floor and ceiling replicated each other into eternity. We noticed that many of the spectators were frightened to step out on to the glass floor. I was scared too. It seemed like a leap out over infinity–you would surely plummet down the lift shaft of eternity. But Rosa had no fear. She leapt at once straight on to the middle of the floor with a flourish of laughter, unafraid to be suspended over nothingness.

So the great prison machine had failed to crush the life out of her. Still her identity flashed between the mirrors. Her leap *was* the moment of identity, the triumph of the momentary, vulnerable 'I'.

Notes

1.   Spengler, Oswald (1930), *The Decline of the West,* (London: George Allen and Unwin pp. 245–246, 251)

2.   Beaton, Cecil (1954), *The Glass of Fashion,* (London: Weidenfeld and Nicolson pp. 120, 304–306, 338)

3.   Sartre, Jean-Paul (1969), *Being and Nothingness,* (London: Methuen p. 607)

4.   Lahr, John (1980), *Prick Up Your Ears,* (Harmondsworth: Penguin pp. 135–136)

5.   Holtby, Winifred (1935), *Women in a Changing Civilization* (reprint 1978, Chicago: Cassandra Editions Academy Ltd p. 148)

6.   Wallis, Jan (1974), 'Why I laughed when Anna was born' in Allen, Sandra, Sanders, Lee and Wallis, Jan, eds (1974), *Conditions of Illusion: Papers from the Women's Movement,* (Leeds: Feminist Books p. 19)

7.   Wickes, George (1977), *The Amazon of Letters,* (London: W H Allen pp. 255, 257, 258)

8.   Meulenbelt, Anja (1980) *The Shame is Over,* (London: The Women's Press)

Virago

If you would like to know more about Virago books, write to us at Ely House, 37 Dover Street, London W1X 4HS for a full catalogue.

Please send a stamped addressed envelope